CW00666684

Trauma and Recovery

A TRAINING PROGRAMME

Kate Cairns and Eileen Fursland

This training programme comprises one-day courses on:

- **Trauma**
- **Resilience**
- **Healing environments**

AKAMAS

BAAF
ADOPTION
& FOSTERING

Published by
British Association for Adoption & Fostering
(BAAF)
Saffron House
6–10 Kirby Street
London EC1N 8TS

www.baaf.org.uk

Charity registration 275689

© Kate Cairns, 2007

British Library Cataloguing in Publication Data

A catalogue record for this book is available from the British Library

ISBN 978 1 905664 16 0

Project management by Shaila Shah, Director of Publications, BAAF
Designed by Andrew Haig & Associates
Typeset by Avon DataSet Ltd, Bidford on Avon
Printed in Great Britain by the Lavenham Press

Trade distribution by Turnaround Publisher Services, Unit 3,
Olympia Trading Estate, Coburg Road, London N22 6TZ

All rights reserved. Apart from any fair dealing for the purposes
of research or private study, or criticism or review, as permitted
under the Copyright, Designs and Patents Act 1988, this publication
may not be reproduced, stored in a retrieval system, or transmitted
in any form or by any means, without the prior written permission
of the publishers.

The moral right of the author has been asserted in accordance
with the Copyright, Designs and Patents Act 1988.

Contents

Notes about the authors

Kate Cairns is a social worker and social work teacher. With her partner, Brian, and their three birth children, she provided permanence for a group of 12 looked after children, all of whom are now adult. She and Brian recently founded Akamas, a training organisation which provides online training for foster carers – www.akamas.co.uk. Kate is also the author of *Attachment, Trauma and Resilience: Therapeutic caring for children*, and *Learn the Child: Helping looked after children to learn* (with Chris Stanway), both published by BAAF.

Eileen Fursland is a professional freelance writer. She has written a number of books and feature stories for magazines, amongst them *Preparing to Adopt: A training pack for preparation groups* for BAAF (alongside a BAAF working party) and *A Guide for Medical Advisers: Advocating, promoting and protecting the health of looked after children in Scotland* (with Ian Millar), both published by BAAF.

Introduction

What this course will do

This course has been designed to help social workers, staff in residential homes, foster carers and adoptive parents to understand more about the needs of traumatised children.

Most foster carers and prospective adoptive parents will attend a general preparation course, during which they will learn something about the effects of neglect and abuse on children. *Trauma and Recovery* goes into much more detail than is possible in a general preparation course. It looks at the long-term effects of trauma on child development and on aspects of a child's life. It also explains how carers can help children to adapt to the developmental impairments they have suffered; build resilience in a traumatised child; and provide an environment that will enhance healing.

Why carers need this course

Children's experiences in early life may have lasting effects on the way they think, feel, perceive and respond to the world and to other people. Children who have suffered neglect, rejection or emotional, physical or sexual abuse often behave in ways that seem inexplicable to other people. Overwhelming stress damages their developing brain and affects their physical, emotional, social and cognitive development in countless ways. Trauma shapes their personality. Without help to recover, they can remain haunted by their experiences for many years, perhaps even a lifetime.

From an inability to concentrate, sleep problems and hyperactivity through to rage, aggression, self-harm and a complete failure to empathise with other people, post-traumatic stress can manifest itself in many different types of behaviour. Much of this behaviour is difficult and challenging, not only for the child herself, but also for those who look after and live with her. It can be extremely taxing, emotionally and physically, and can leave carers feeling bruised and confused too. Some placements break down under the strain.

Foster carers and adoptive parents who take on the tough job of caring for such troubled children need and deserve the best help available. Agencies owe it to carers to prepare them as well as possible. This will help carers not only to cope day-to-day but also to provide the kind of care which gives the child the best chance of recovering from her experiences and building the resilience to cope with life's challenges.

Understanding the effects of stress and trauma gives foster carers and adoptive parents insight into why troubled children behave as they do. It helps them to interpret the child's words and actions in a different light; it also means they can help *the child himself* to understand why he feels and behaves the way he does.

Carers cannot erase those early distressing or horrifying experiences, but they can learn how to help the child recover from post-traumatic stress disorders. With the right help, children can stabilise, integrate, adapt and gain self-esteem, a sense of social connectedness and the capacity for joy.

This course explains how.

How to use these training materials

The course works best with groups of between 8 and 20 participants.

It covers three subjects: **trauma**, **resilience after trauma** and **healing environments**. The material in this pack contains Powerpoint presentations for each of these three subjects – two sessions on each subject, making six sessions in all.

Trauma:
- Attachment, trauma and child development
- Helping children to recover from and adapt to acquired impairments

Resilience after trauma:
- Understanding resilience after trauma
- Building on strengths in the child and the social network

Healing environments:
- What is a healing environment?
- Planning the healing environment

The training can be delivered flexibly in several different ways, depending on what works best for the agency and participants. It could be given:
- as three separate full-day courses on trauma, resilience and healing environments (separated by days, weeks or months)
- as a three-day course, with one subject each day on consecutive days
- as six separate sessions (perhaps delivered in the evenings or at weekends)

The training has been designed so that the timing can be flexible. Each session lasts around three hours, although this can vary either way. If the agency wants the trainer to go into the subjects in more depth, there is the option to spend longer on discussion and training exercises. A single session could be delivered in an evening. Alternatively it could be given in one day, allowing more time for discussion and training exercises. This could start at 10am and end at 3.15pm, which allows time for a coffee break and a lunch break, finishing in time to allow participants to collect children from school. With an earlier start and a later finish, two sessions could be combined in one day of training if necessary.

Participants often learn a great deal from hearing about other people's experiences. This is why the course includes a number of training exercises in which participants work in small groups, sharing their ideas and thoughts, often feeding back the key points to the rest of the group. These training exercises and discussions are valuable elements of the learning, so should be included if at all possible. But if time is short, trainers can use their discretion and keep the training exercises brief or even omit some of them. Coffee breaks or the lunch break can also be used as discussion times.

What this pack includes

- a CD-ROM containing a **PowerPoint presentation** and a set of **handouts**. The handouts may be printed out and photocopied for distribution to participants attending the course; they may not be used for other purposes and BAAF retains the copyright unless otherwise indicated.

- this **book**, which contains the following:
  - reproductions of the PowerPoint slide presentation for each of the six sessions (each presentation includes the learning outcomes for that session);
  - supplementary material to help the trainer to comment further on the points made on the slides;
  - suggested training exercises, usually for small group work, to encourage participants to share their thoughts, ideas and experiences and to encourage reflection and learning;

- suggested questions which the trainer can raise with the group, briefly and informally, at certain points in the presentation.

What you will need

- A flipchart with paper

- A laptop computer with CD-ROM drive and PowerPoint

- A screen for displaying PowerPoint slides

- Pens, pencils and coloured crayons for participants to use

Venue

Ideally, this course should be held in a venue that is well-heated, well-lit and comfortable, and that feels welcoming. You will need adequate seating for participants and access to tables will be helpful. You will probably want somewhere that provides refreshments or that has provision for making drinks. If you are presenting this course in full-day sessions, you will also need somewhere which provides lunch or which provides opportunities for participants to buy lunch, or bring lunch with them and eat it in the venue. You will need to think about whether your venue is easily accessible to carers. Is it on good transport routes? Is there disabled access? Parking? Is there a crèche?

Evaluation

On the CD-ROM, an evaluation form is provided for participants to complete and return. This is important for the course leaders, your organisation and for the carers themselves. Evaluation allows the service users to voice their opinions of the training, and contribute to improvements in its provision, and it provides you and your organisation with invaluable feedback about the impact and effectiveness of what you do.

How to run training groups

Preparation

The course can be delivered by a single trainer, ideally someone with experience in the area of fostering or adoption. Agencies should ensure that course leaders:

- have the necessary training skills;

- have an understanding of adult learning principles;

- are committed to anti-discriminatory practice;

- are familiar with the course content and are confident in delivering this.

It would help trainers a great deal in delivering this course if they have read *Attachment, Trauma and Resilience: Therapeutic caring for children* by Kate Cairns (BAAF, 2002).

Dealing with difficult issues

Every one of us has been a child. We know what it is like to be a child and to be frightened, or lonely, or sad, or angry. Every childhood has its share of such experiences. Some of us also know what it is like to be a child and to be rejected, neglected or abused. Adults who can connect with the experiences of childhood, who have processed any harmful experiences in their past and can contain the powerful feelings evoked, are often the people best placed to work with children. As a trainer, you need to emphasise the value of everyone's prior life experience, whether they have experienced childhood trauma or worked with traumatised children or not.

This course will invite and expect participants to reflect on their own experience as well as the experience of traumatised children. They need to be prepared for the thoughts and feelings that may emerge when they think about these issues. During the discussions some participants may share their children's stories of neglect and abuse. There may be some people in the group who find these stories distressing – perhaps because it upsets them to think of this happening to any child or perhaps because it brings back memories of something that happened to them or someone they loved. As a trainer, you will need to be aware of this possibility and be prepared to help acknowledge and deal with painful emotions. You need to help participants realise that, although they are on the course because they care for other people, they also need to take care of themselves. You will be discussing stress and relaxation a lot – sometimes it is helpful if carers think about these issues in relation to themselves as well as the children and young people they look after.

Reflective discussion and training exercises

Asking participants about their own views and experiences encourages open discussion, shows them how much they already know and allows them to learn from each other. However, trainers should feel free to include different training exercises or bring up other points for discussion if they feel these would work better with their particular group of participants.

Group dynamics

In any group of people, there will be some who say a lot and some who say very little; some who are dominant and appear to have all the answers, and others who seem to have little confidence in the value of their own views and experiences.

Some people feel uncomfortable with the material and individuals have different ways of dealing with this. While there is a place for humour even on a course like this, you may find your group contains someone who feels the need to be "the life and soul of the party". Experience teaches teachers and trainers ways in which they can diplomatically handle participants who never seem to stop talking or never miss the opportunity to crack a joke.

Some participants may be very experienced in fostering traumatised children; others may feel almost as though they have no right to be on the course because they are still waiting for a child to be placed with them. Some may be managing well with the child or young person placed with them; others will be struggling and feeling inadequate. Every trainer has his or her own teaching style, but whatever your individual style, it is your responsibility to put people at their ease, encourage everyone to make a contribution and help the group "gel". You need to be sensitive to the way the individuals within the group are feeling. If necessary, you may have to tactfully encourage this sensitivity among certain participants in the group as well.

Be aware of what is going on in the small groups as they work together. If one or two groups are being dominated by particular individuals or you can see personalities clashing, mix up the groups in different ways. People learn in different ways, so it is not necessary for everyone to speak out the whole time in order to get value from the course – but do make sure that every participant has the space and opportunity to speak and ask questions if they want to. Sometimes one participant gets "hung up" on a particular issue or question and doesn't want to let it drop. 'Let's talk more about this later over coffee – we have a lot to fit in and I think we need to move on now' is one way to handle this.

Diversity issues

It is your responsibility to ensure that the course is accessible to everyone and that all participants – whatever their ethnic background, sexuality or educational level – feel equally valued, respected and able to contribute. As a trainer, you need to be sensitive to the composition of the group and consider how you will include and address the needs of participants who are from minority ethnic groups, who have a disability, who are single or gay or lesbian.

If any participants have disabilities, check the accessibility of the building and the layout of the room and, if necessary, make sure a parking space will be available for them close to the building. Asking participants in advance about any disabilities will forewarn you about the need for a British Sign Language interpreter or the need to provide handouts in a larger type size, for instance.

When setting dates for training, be careful not to clash with any religious holidays.

The course may be targeted at a particular ethnic group – in which case you may of course deliver the course in the appropriate language. In other cases, where necessary, consider the need for interpreters to work alongside the trainer.

When setting ground rules at the start of the course, make it clear to all the participants that you will challenge any discriminatory attitudes or remarks. You may wish to tackle the issues head-on, for example, by stating that your agency values gay men and lesbians who can offer care and stability to children, just as much as it values heterosexual people – either single people or couples – who can do the same.

First things first

Every time you give the course to a new group or to the same group in a different venue:

- Start by introducing yourself.

- Explain the arrangements for the day: what time and where you will be having refreshments and lunch, and what time the course will finish.

- Ask if anyone will need to leave before the end of the course.

- Tell participants where the toilets are and what to do if the fire alarm sounds.

- Make sure everyone can see you (and the screen) and hear you.

- Make sure participants are comfortable with the room temperature.

- Ask them to turn their mobile phones to "silent".

- Talk about issues such as confidentiality and the sensitivity of the subject matter.

- Give participants a handout of the slide presentation so they do not need to write everything down.

How this course came about

I am a social worker and social work teacher. My partner Brian and I, along with our three birth children, fostered 12 children over a 25-year period. Between 1975 and 2000, in our large family home in rural Gloucestershire, which was provided by a charitable trust, we offered permanence to the children as part of our family group. The children joined the family at various stages of their childhood, ranging in age from 4 to 15. The children had all experienced overwhelming stress in early life. Between them they displayed all the rage, fear, grief and disturbed, destructive and self-destructive behaviours that so often follow attachment difficulties, loss, abuse and trauma.

The knowledge and experience that we gained as we responded to the children's difficulties and helped promote their recovery forms the foundation of this training material. We built on our experience of the realities of family life with traumatised children by drawing on knowledge and ideas absorbed from theory and research. We developed a model which explains how stress damages the brain – a model which also provides for healing and recovery. We showed that, in the right conditions and with the right help, children can learn to adapt to the impairments and difficulties that are the legacy of overwhelming stress. A fulfilled and happy life need not be beyond their reach.

All of our foster children are now grown up. Almost all remain in contact with us and most are in regular and frequent contact.

Brian and I went on to form a company, Akamas Training, to share our knowledge and expertise with foster carers, social workers and other professionals working in the field. Akamas provides online training for social workers, foster carers and others who work with traumatised children. It provides a route to two qualifications in foster care, a BTEC Advanced Certificate and a BTEC Professional Certificate – delivered and assessed online. Akamas also runs one-day training courses.

BAAF wanted to make this valuable training more widely available to foster carers and social workers across the UK. So, working in partnership, BAAF and Akamas have adapted the online learning material into courses that agencies themselves can deliver, in a flexible way, to meet the training needs of their foster carers, prospective adoptive parents and social workers. Such training can stand alone, or can complement the online BTEC qualifications.

Kate Cairns

1 Trauma

Attachment, trauma and child development

Setting the scene

This is the first session of the course, so welcome the participants, introduce yourself and put them at their ease.

Explain what they can expect from the course – that there will be some direct input from you, in terms of your slide presentation, but that they also have a lot to contribute from their own knowledge and experience. Explain that they will not simply be sitting and listening to you – they will be actively involved in discussion and group exercises, coming up with their own thoughts, ideas and suggestions.

Also briefly explain the context to the learning material and how it came to be developed, referring to Kate Cairns' experience and expertise (as detailed in the introductory material).

Acknowledge that learning more about the abuse and neglect that some children suffer can be shocking and upsetting. For some participants it may even bring back unhappy memories of their own childhoods and these feelings can be difficult to cope with. Everyone needs to be sensitive to the fact that some participants may have traumatic experiences in their past. Some may be keen to share this with the group; others may dread having to refer to it at all. Reassure people that they will not be asked to share any information that they would rather keep to themselves.

Introductions

Ask participants to introduce themselves to the rest of the group. If this is the start of a three-day course, you might want to have more extended introductions, for instance, asking the participants to talk about why they are here and what they hope to gain from the course.

Establish ground rules

Invite participants to suggest some rules for how people should behave on the training course. Write these suggestions on a flip chart and leave them visible for the rest of the course. The points might include, for instance:

- Turn off mobile phones or at least put them on "silent" mode.

- Keep confidential everything that people share within the group about their or their children's experiences.

- Respect difference. Participants come from a variety of backgrounds and have a range of perspectives. Everyone should respect these differences.

- Don't be afraid to ask questions.

- If anyone disagrees with what someone else has said, they should challenge the statement but respect the person.

- Listen to others as well as talking about your own views and experiences.

Provide the handout

Give participants a handout of the slide presentation so that they do not need to write everything down – they can make additional notes on their handout if this is helpful.

The presentation

SLIDE 1 Attachment, trauma and child development

Patterns laid down in babyhood are significant for the child's later personality and behaviour. When older children present with behaviours that are puzzling, you may ask yourself: 'How did that come about?' This session will try to help you answer that question, particularly in relation to children who have been neglected, rejected or abused early in life.

Many children who have been traumatised will never remember the traumatic experience, although it may haunt them forever because it changes their development in a number of ways: biological, psychological and social. It can result in complex disorders that have much in common with other conditions and developmental impairments.

A child may have survived trauma that is fully known and recorded; or she may have survived trauma that she can remember but has never told anyone about. Or she may have survived trauma that she cannot remember and that no one around her – social workers, foster family, teachers – knows about.

In all these cases post-traumatic stress can affect the child's development and her physical, psychological and social functioning. If the people around the child know about the traumatic events, they may recognise that her problems are due to the effects of trauma. If they don't know about the trauma, they may attribute the disorders to some other cause, from genetic impairment to criminality.

This session will help you to understand the effects of overwhelming stress on a baby's developing brain and how the long-term effects of stress and trauma can impair a child's development and behaviour in many different areas in her everyday life.

SLIDE 2 Learning outcomes

- **Recognise impact of overwhelming stress on child development**
- **Relate self-regulation of stress, mood and impulse to behaviour in childhood**
- **Think about strategies to enable children to recover from acquired developmental impairments . . .**
- **. . . and to promote resilience by enabling children to adapt to these impairments**

This slide shows the learning outcomes for sessions A and B – *Attachment, trauma and child development*, and *Helping children to recover from and adapt to acquired impairments*.

Explain that what this really means is that, by the end of the course, participants will understand more about traumatised children and why they behave as they do. They will also know more about what they themselves, as carers, can do on a day-to-day basis to promote their child's recovery from post-traumatic stress disorder.

SLIDE 3   What is attachment?

- Attachment is an affectional bond between humans
- The feelings involved may be constructive or destructive
- Babies can only gain control of their own survival by gaining control of their carers
- Dependency and control are key elements of infant attachment

An "affectional bond" does not mean a bond that involves showing or feeling affection. It means it involves "affect", which is the psychologists' term for any kind of feelings. Babies build relationships, or become attached, to other humans through strong feelings they have for them. The strong feelings may be of love but in other cases they could be of anger or fear. These relationships affect the way babies' brains develop.

The same thing can happen to adults – there is a well-known phenomenon called Stockholm Syndrome, in which hostages develop a distorted perception of reality and feelings of attachment and loyalty to their captors.

If a baby's early attachment relationships are distorted, he may develop issues of dependency and control. You may have come across a child who has a deep need to be in control; these children do whatever they can to provoke a reaction in you or get you to discipline them so that they can feel 'I made that happen'.

Question: Have any of you cared for a child like this? In what way did the child try to gain control? How did you handle it?

SLIDE 4   Brain development

The brain develops sequentially:
- **Brain stem** – state regulation
  Before birth – eight months
- **Mid-brain** – motor functioning
  Birth – one year
- **Limbic brain** – emotional functioning
  Six months – two years
- **Cortex** – cognitive functioning
  One year – four years

Compared with other mammals, humans have large brains. But human babies are born with relatively undeveloped brains – most brain development takes place after birth. This means that brain development is affected by what happens to the baby in the first years of life. And the single most important factor is the quality of the baby's relationships.

SLIDE 5   Claiming: attention, bonding, control and dependency

- Human babies are born utterly helpless
- They are dependent for everything on their carers
- To survive they must gain control of their carers
- Control is always an infantile response
- As babies develop a sense of safety they become less controlling
- Older children with unmet needs may be very needy with issues of attention, control and dependency

In order to survive, a baby needs a carer who is committed. If the baby does not have a carer who meets his needs, he will die. So gaining "control" of the carers is vital for a baby. Once the baby trusts that his needs will be met reliably, there is less need to "control" the carers.

 Question: Can you suggest any circumstances in which a carer might not reliably meet a baby's needs?

When the carer is not meeting a baby's needs, perhaps because of a drug addiction, chaotic lifestyle or mental health problems, the baby never learns that her carers will look after her; she never develops a sense of safety. In later childhood, these children may be very attention-seeking and driven to try to control people. As a carer, you feel that their needs are so great that you will never be able to meet them. We have to find ways to help the child fill that gap.

SLIDE 6   Attunement

- Babies and carers engage in an intimate dance conversation
- Their bodies and brains, feelings and thoughts begin to work in tune
- This attunement patterns the infant brain
- Stimulation and relaxation is the first pattern
- Attunement provides a blueprint for all human interaction
- Children who did not have these needs met as babies may be unable to regulate stress

Attunement is a very physical process. It is important for babies. A baby will feel stress when he is hot, cold, uncomfortable or frightened. Usually, when a baby is stressed, he cries, which produces stress in the carer. The carer will then respond by meeting the baby's need.

 Question: What is the first thing we usually do when a baby is crying?

The first step is usually to pick up the baby and soothe her by rocking or patting her, or crooning. Then the carer will feed the baby or change her nappy or make sure she is warm enough.

These actions have the effect of reducing the carer's stress level so that breathing slows down and the muscles relax. The baby follows suit. This pattern forms a link between soothing activity and physical relaxation. As the baby stops crying and relaxes, the carer produces endorphins (pleasure hormones) and pheromones (chemicals produced by the skin when the body chemistry changes). Again, the baby follows suit. This repeated cycle builds a pattern in the baby's brain in which stress is eased by soothing and relaxing. But some babies do not have the opportunity to learn to regulate stress. Their carers do not reliably meet their needs or teach them this pattern of soothing and relaxing after stress. In these cases, as the brain develops, continued unregulated stress may damage the brain.

SLIDE 7 — Hyperarousal and dissociation

- When in early life adults do not enable the baby to regulate stress, the child will either remain hyperaroused or will dissociate
- Hyperaroused children show extreme reactions to stimuli
- Dissociated children show minimal reactions to stimuli
- In either case the unregulated stress will be causing injury

When the adults in the baby's life do not reliably soothe him and attunement is lacking, one of two things can happen. The baby may remain in a continuously stressed state, which means he will continue to feel uncomfortable, afraid or unhappy over a prolonged period. This is known as "hyperarousal" and a child who is hyperaroused will show extreme reactions to stimuli.

Alternatively he may "dissociate" or "cut off" from these feelings, which means he may no longer be aware of feeling uncomfortable or afraid and will seem to react little to external stimuli.

In both cases, however, the stress hormones are still present in the child's body and have a damaging effect on his brain.

SLIDE 8 — Behavioural indicators in babies

- Hyperarousal:
  - Perpetual crying
  - Gaze aversion
  - Exaggerated startle response
  - Touch aversion
  - Feeding problems
  - Tense muscle tone
- Dissociation:
  - Minimal crying
  - Dominant gaze
  - Minimal startle response
  - Unresponsive to touch
  - Feeding problems
  - Floppy muscle tone

These are some of the signs that a baby is either hyperaroused or dissociated. A baby who is hyperaroused is over-responsive to stimulation, which can make touch and even eye contact too stimulating to be comfortable. She may try to avoid looking at people and will not like to be touched or cuddled. She seems jumpy and will cry a lot.

Older children who are suffering the effects of trauma may be completely unable to look someone in the eye. Teachers who are telling them off may often say: 'Look at me when I'm talking to you!' without realising that, rather than being rude, the child actually finds eye contact profoundly uncomfortable and is unable to tolerate it.

Children who are dissociated, on the other hand, may have an extremely dominant gaze which can be quite disconcerting for those on the receiving end. They do not respond much to any kind of stimulation such as sound and touch; they rarely cry and seem "floppy", with little muscle tone. They often have feeding problems – a dissociated child may gorge on food, not recognising the sensations of fullness, or may use eating or not eating as a way of controlling adults.

Question: Do you recognise any of these signs in the children you are looking after or have looked after?

SLIDE 9   Developmental trauma

- Trauma means injury
- Unregulated stress causes injury to the brain
- Children with unmet attachment needs often cannot regulate stress
- Injuries acquired through stress dysregulation because of unmet infant attachment needs may be described as developmental trauma

As we have seen, when a baby does not learn how to calm himself down when stressed, the continued production of stress hormones has a damaging effect on the brain. Children who have not been able to become attached to their parent or carer – perhaps because the parent or carer has been unavailable, unreliable or neglectful – have unmet needs and often cannot regulate their own stress. The damaging effects of this on a child's brain are described as "developmental trauma". It affects the way the child thinks, feels and behaves.

SLIDE 10   Emotional trauma

- Once children can process feelings and can think, they may be injured through exposure to terrifying events
- Such events lead to extreme stress which injures the brain
- Injuries acquired through exposure to overwhelming fear or horror may be described as emotional trauma

As we have seen, children who have not been able to benefit from the attachment process and develop stress regulation suffer lasting effects from this. And children who have lived through traumatic experiences will also have been injured in their ability to regulate stress.

When something happens that terrifies a child – and something that is terrifying for a child may not be the same as for an adult – and the child is old enough to think and process feelings, she experiences extreme fear or horror. This leads to extreme stress, which has a damaging effect on the brain. Stress "turns off" the blood supply to certain areas of the brain. Again, this injury affects the way the child thinks, feels and behaves – and this is described as "emotional trauma".

Even when they did develop stress regulation in their early years, children who go through trauma often lose that ability.

Children are more vulnerable than adults. They are developmentally immature. And if they experience trauma it is often complex and repeated trauma, which means the damage to the brain is happening again and again over a long period. The field trials for the *Diagnostic and Statistical Manual (DSM) of Mental Disorders* found that the most complex, severe and persistent disorders after trauma are those that follow traumatic experience in the first decade of life.

SLIDE 11   **Defining primary trauma: DSM IV***

- Trauma is:
  - an event which is, or is realistically perceived to be, threatening to the life or personal integrity of self or others *AND*
  - the response to the event is one of fear, helplessness or horror

This slide shows the medical definition of trauma. Trauma is a psychological event but it results from an external event, for instance, the child may be beaten or threatened with death.

 Question: Can you think of any other kinds of external event, other than physical or sexual abuse, which could cause trauma to a child?

Emotional abuse can be as threatening to the child's personal integrity, and as likely to cause trauma to the child, as physical or sexual abuse. It is the distortion of the emotional relationship which is terrifying to the child.

Note that trauma is an event which is threatening to the life or personal integrity of the self *or others* – because humans are social beings and we are interdependent, we can be traumatised by witnessing the violation of other people. A child who witnesses an act of violence or domestic violence is still damaged by this, even if she herself is not attacked.

SLIDE 12   **Traumatic stress**

- The automatic response to trauma, involving the production of toxic amounts of stress hormones which affect:
  - brain function
  - all major body systems
  - social functioning
- A *bio-psycho-social* injury

 Question: How do we react when faced with a life-threatening situation?

At a time when a dangerous and threatening situation demands "fight or flight", we humans don't stop to think through all the options, we simply respond instinctively, in the way animals do. Large amounts of stress hormones flood the brain. This affects all major systems of the body – for instance, oxygen is diverted to the muscles, so that we can run away quickly; we may empty our bladder or bowels; we may be unable to speak or even scream. Traumatic stress also affects brain function, in that the blood supply to certain parts of the brain is stopped. This means that certain brain cells die.

Children who have lived through traumatic stress and have been unable to recover spontaneously may suffer impairment as a result. Such impairment is global in its effects; it has an impact on every aspect of functioning in daily life.

* The *Diagnostic and Statistical Manual of Mental Disorders* (fourth edition) (DSM IV), published by the American Psychiatric Association, is a diagnostic reference of mental health professionals in the United States. It includes diagnostic criteria for the most common mental disorders, including description, diagnosis, treatment, and research findings.

NB Refer participants to the diagram, Traumatic stress and brain function, in the handout titled Trauma (this is on the CD-ROM).

SLIDE 13   # Conditions necessary for recovery

- **Safety**
- **Supportive social network with secure attachment relationships**
- **The ability to express what has happened**

In some cases the damage can be repaired as the brain forms new connections. A process of recovery is possible after traumatic stress, but it can only happen if certain conditions are met.

In order to recover from traumatic stress, we need:

- to feel safe;

- to have the support of people we are attached to;

- to be able to express the traumatic event.

This is why a child may still be suffering the effects of trauma by the time she comes to you to be fostered or adopted. If children have not had these three conditions met in their lives so far, they are unlikely to have started the process of recovery.

SLIDE 14   # The phases of spontaneous recovery

- **Stabilisation**
  - **Establishing a sense of security in a safe environment**

- **Integration**
  - **Regaining physiological self-management**
  - **Processing events through attachment relationships**
  - **Checking perceptions of reality**

- **Adaptation**
  - **Who am I now that I have changed?**
  - **Regaining self-esteem**
  - **Rediscovering the experience of joy**

During the first few years of life the brain is developing and stabilising, and young children are integrating all their experience into a narrative or life story that enables them to function so that they are personally and socially adaptable and resilient. This process takes place through the secure attachments they have with attuned adults.

But the injuries that result from traumatic stress cause:

- destabilisation;

- disintegration.

If the victim is able to recover spontaneously they will:

- stabilise;

- integrate what has happened to them into their life story;

- adapt to being a changed person, who sees the world differently.

This is what happens in the three phases of recovery:

Stabilisation:

- We need not only to be safe, but to feel safe.

- We need to learn about the impact of our experience.

- We need to learn or relearn words for feelings.

Integration:

- We need to get back the ability to manage our stress.

- We have to be able to "process" what has happened to us by talking to the people we love.

- We need to make sure that our perceptions of reality are correct, because trauma distorts the thought processes.

- Abuse or trauma can shape children's thinking in a number of ways, e.g. they may have come to believe that whatever happened was their own fault, that people who love them will always abuse them, or that nothing good can ever happen to them.

 Question: can you suggest some ways in which a child's thinking might have been shaped by abuse or trauma?

Adaptation:

- When we have recovered we still have to adapt – we have to rethink who we are and how we relate to things and people after experiencing a life-changing event.

- We have to regain our self-esteem after perhaps blaming ourselves or feeling worthless or guilty.

- We have to re-learn the ability to enjoy life – the pleasure response in the brain may have been "turned off" for a long time.

SLIDE 15 Lasting effects of unresolved traumatic stress injuries

- **Children who have lived through traumatic stress may experience functional impairment as a result**
- **The impairment is the result of the bio-psycho-social injury**
- **Such impairment is global in its effects**
- **It can occur in children with no prior impairment**
- **The effects are more complex and persistent in children with prior impairment**

The effects of traumatic stress can be long-lasting for children and affect every aspect of their lives. It can affect their development in many different ways. In the case of a child who was already experiencing some kind of impairment due to stress, a traumatic event is likely to affect him in more complex ways, and for longer, than a child who was not previously damaged by stress.

SLIDE 16   Examples of functional impairment

- Effects on brain development and function
- Physiological effects
- Physical effects
- Emotional effects
- Social effects

This functional impairment can affect many different aspects of the child's everyday life, the way she feels and thinks and behaves, and the way she responds to people and events.

Exercise: the effects of trauma on the child

Leaving Slide 16 on display, ask participants to gather into small groups of about four people. Give them 20 minutes to complete the following exercise.

In small groups, discuss some of the ways you think such effects might be evident in the child's everyday life. What effects do you think there might be on her **brain function**, for instance, in terms of memory and language? How might her experience affect her **physiologically**? For instance, you might expect her to have disturbed sleep or eating patterns. There will also be **physical** effects in terms of her health and **emotional** effects on her mood and her feelings about herself. **Socially**, how do you think the functional impairment might affect her life? Perhaps she might find it difficult to make friends or to trust people.

In your groups, I would like you to come up with as many ideas and examples as you can under each of these five headings and write them on a large piece of flip chart paper.

If you are looking after a traumatised child – or you have done so in the past – you may be able to give some specific examples from that child's own experience and the kind of behaviour she displayed. But if not, think about traumatised children in general and how their experience might have affected them in these different ways.

Allow the groups around 20 minutes for discussion and then, in the feedback session, ask each group to present to the other participants the ideas and thoughts they wrote down. To avoid repetition, ask each group to present their ideas for the effects of just one type of functional impairment (brain development, physiological, physical, emotional, social). Then, for each type of impairment, invite the remaining groups to add any other ideas that have not already been suggested by the group that is presenting.

The next five slides will allow you to confirm and elaborate on the ideas which the participants themselves have thought of.

SLIDE 17   Effects on brain development and function

- These functions may be diminished or lost:
  - language, especially spoken language
  - words for feelings
  - sense of meaning and connection
  - empathy
  - impulse control
  - mood regulation
  - short-term memory
  - capacity for joy

The effects on brain development and function are wide-ranging.

- The child's ability to understand or express himself in language, especially spoken language, may be affected. He will probably understand more than he can express. If he uses more than one language; it is usually the mother tongue that is affected.

- He may be unable to tell people how he is feeling; instead, he will "act out" his feelings. He may not actually know *what* he is feeling, because – due to the long-term effects of stress on the brain – feeling is translated directly into action without going through the process of thought.

- He may seem at a loss when it comes to understanding meanings and connections between things – nothing seems to make sense to him. It seems almost as though he is cut off from the world by the "glass wall" of trauma.

- He may lack empathy and appear unable to work out what other people are feeling. On the other hand, some children are very tuned in to trauma in others and seem to make a beeline for children at school who have been similarly affected.

- Under ordinary conditions the brain inhibits our impulses and allows us to think about what we are doing. When there is a threat to our survival, this inhibition turns off so that we can act instantly without stopping to think. In a threatening situation, it is not helpful to spend too much time thinking before we act. When confronted by a sabre-toothed tiger, our primitive ancestor would have the best chance of survival if he followed his immediate impulse to run. When children become disordered after trauma they remain unable to regulate impulse. The part of the brain that enables us to manage impulse and think before we act has been damaged by trauma. Traumatised children do not think before they act – this is why, when asked by a teacher or carer, they find it so hard to explain *why* they did something.

- His mood may be very volatile or very flat. He is predictably unpredictable.

- His short-term memory may be poor – by the time they reach the top of the stairs he may have forgotten what he went up for. These are children who never have the right kit for their lesson at the right time.

- There may be other types of memory disturbance too: children often have difficulty remembering the traumatic events (this is called amnesia). Sometimes children have difficulty forgetting the traumatic events, but are constantly and unintentionally ruminating on what happened to them (hypermnesia).

- For children who have not recovered from emotional trauma, life is flat and there is nothing that gives them real pleasure or joy. For most of us, memories of having fun or being happy will sustain us through other times. But these children do not remember being happy.

 Question: Do any of these signs sound familiar to you?

SLIDE 18 Physiological effects

- **Perpetual extreme levels of stress arousal may lead to:**
  - **hypervigilance and loss of ability to concentrate**
  - **altered vision and hearing**
  - **hyperactivity or dissociation**
  - **avoidance of potential triggers to trauma**
  - **altered sleep patterns**
  - **altered eating patterns**
  - **compulsive self harm**
  - **attempts to self-medicate with substances**

Continued high levels of stress arousal can have effects on the body's physiology too.

- These children may be used to constantly scanning the environment for threats, which may over time lead to reduced focal vision and enhanced peripheral vision – this means they find it hard to focus on what is in front of them (e.g. a school textbook) and may be more attentive to what is going on alongside them or out of the window. This can cause problems in the classroom.

- When the brain is filtering sounds, it usually filters in favour of the human voice. But in children who have suffered traumatic damage, ordinary non-threatening sounds such as their teacher's voice may be filtered out so that they "tune out" after a few minutes.

- In children who are dissociated rather than hyperaroused, the effects of trauma may not be so obvious but these children are still traumatised. It can be quite unsettling for a teacher or carer – it's as though "the lights are on but no one's at home".

- The child may avoid certain places that trigger the memory of the trauma, without even realising what she is doing or why. For instance, suppose a child who has been abused is standing with you, at the checkout queue in the supermarket. She smells the aftershave of the man in front of you in the queue and it is the same aftershave that her abuser used. This can trigger a memory of the abuse without the child even realising why. And she may become afraid of queueing in the supermarket, again without knowing why.

Question: Can you think of any examples of avoidance behaviour in children you are caring for or have cared for?

- At the time of trauma, the body spontaneously generates opioids – chemicals similar to opiate drugs – to try to quell pain. Traumatised children may later turn to self-harming behaviour such as cutting in order to trigger the release of these opioids again, in a "maintenance dose". Or they may start self-harming because they believe they deserve to be hurt, or because they are dissociated and are resorting to desperate measures in an attempt to feel something.

- Traumatised children often attempt to "self-medicate" with various substances such as alcohol or illegal drugs. Because they have difficult feelings which they cannot do anything about – having never developed the ability to regulate their stress – this is their way of trying to either dull their feelings or, in dissociated children, to produce some kind of feeling.

- Hyperaroused children become addicted to their own stress hormones. They may come to demand a high stimulus environment – with lots of noise and activity and attention – because they suffer withdrawal symptoms in a low stimulus environment. Adults often feed into this adverse pattern by meeting the demand for constant stimulation, which in fact is on a law of diminishing returns. It is important to help children live with the discomfort of a low stimulus environment rather than provide the excessive stimulus they demand.

SLIDE 19   **Physical effects**

- Continued stress arousal may lead to:
  - headaches
  - digestive disorders
  - respiratory disorders
  - other psychosomatic illnesses
  - muscle tension
  - aching joints
  - clumsiness
  - altered spatial awareness

Continued stress has physical effects. We have all heard of psychosomatic illness. Feelings of fear, anxiety and sorrow that the child cannot express may manifest themselves as sickness or diarrhoea or other conditions. Sometimes this is obvious – for instance, if the child's illnesses tend to occur around the time of contact with birth relatives.

 Question: Have you come across a child who experiences psychosomatic illness?

SLIDE 20   **Emotional effects**

- **Loss of ability to process experience through language**
- **Diminished or lost capacity for empathy**
- **Hypersensitivity to trauma in others**
- **Diminished range of emotions: terror or rage**
- **Loss of capacity for joy leads to diminished aesthetic and spiritual experience**
- **Feelings of worthlessness and shame**
- **Traumatic stress takes over core identity**

Trauma can have dramatic effects on the child's emotional world.

- The child may lose the ability to process his experience through language – in other words, he literally can't tell you how he is feeling.

- He may have difficulty understanding how other people feel or why they react the way they do – except in the case of other people who have been similarly traumatised. He does not experience the full range of emotions himself and may be emotionally flat apart from when he is terrified or flying into a rage.

- He does not seem to experience the wonder that other children often feel. When a child relates to the world with pleasure and excitement, this is satisfying and pleasing for other people around him. But a child who does not experience joy can be depressing to live with. You feel that nothing you do gives him any pleasure or enjoyment.

- His self-esteem may be low and he feels worthless and ashamed.

- There is a phenomenon known as "traumatic identity", in which a person's core beliefs are all based around the experience of trauma. For instance, 'I deserve to be hurt'; 'People who love me always abuse me'; 'It's dangerous for me to be happy'.

Question: can you think of any ways you could help a child to understand that these kind of beliefs are mistaken? How could you help the child to develop alternative thoughts and beliefs?

SLIDE 21   Social effects

- Diminished impulse control may lead to social isolation or membership of deviant peer group
- Extreme reactions of terror or rage frighten others
- Diminished empathy limits social connectedness
- Being in survival mode restricts motivation to be sociable, except with other victims of trauma
- Avoidance restricts capacity to connect to others or to the sensory environment
- Diminished language functions restrict social accountability
- Taking on traumatic identity leads to persistent victim or aggressor behaviour

Difficulties with emotions and behaviour have an impact on social life.

- Because traumatised children have difficulty controlling their impulses, their behaviour is – literally – impulsive. They behave unpredictably and their lack of inhibition can lead to difficult behaviour such as crime and aggression. This in turn may mean they are socially isolated – other children are afraid of them and avoid them. Sometimes the child may become part of a deviant peer group whose other members also have behaviour problems or are deemed "daring" or "hard".

- The child's tendency to fly into a rage can be frightening for other children, and indeed adults. Their rage can be completely uncontrolled, like a toddler tantrum.

- Often these children cannot connect with other people, no matter how hard they try. Their traumatised state means they may have little motivation to make friendships – except perhaps with other victims of trauma, whom they may recognise as kindred spirits.

- The avoidance techniques they use will prevent them from fully entering into what is going on around them, whether in the classroom or in social settings. They have not learned – or have lost the capacity for – the give and take of social interaction, of talking about themselves and listening to others.

- Bullies will always find victims and traumatised children may be ready victims. Alternatively, they may have identified with their aggressors in the past and take on the role of the bully themselves.

Question: Do any of these signs sound familiar to you from your experience of caring for a traumatised child?

SLIDE 22   The three phases of treatment

- **Stabilisation**
  - Safety
  - Learning about trauma
  - Learning or relearning words for feelings
- **Integration**
  - Physiological self-management
  - Emotional processing
  - Cognitive restructuring
- **Adaptaton**
  - Establishing social connectedness
  - Developing self-esteem
  - Discovering or rediscovering the experience of joy

As we have seen, in the right conditions, children who have suffered trauma can recover spontaneously. But in many cases the conditions for recovery are not present, which means some children suffer lasting effects from unresolved traumatic stress injuries. Recovery is still possible, with the help of skilled and knowledgeable people who understand the effects of traumatic stress and how to treat it.

In order to recover after trauma, however long after the event, children will need to:

- stabilise;

- integrate their experience into their "life story" and make sense of their world;

- develop adaptive responses and let go of maladaptive responses.

In the next session we will learn about how we, as carers, can help a child go through these processes so that she can recover and adapt and have new hope after suffering overwhelming stress.

SESSION B

Helping children to recover from and adapt to acquired impairments

SLIDE 23 **Helping children to recover from and adapt to acquired impairments**

This slide introduces Session B

As we saw in the first session, traumatic stress affects brain development. The child may recover spontaneously, in the right conditions: safety; a supportive social network with secure attachment relationships; and the ability to express what has happened. Without these conditions, he may need skilled and knowledgeable adults to help him recover from long-term disorder resulting from the trauma. Either way, the processes are the same. He needs to:

- stabilise – i.e. feel safe, learn about trauma, learn words to express how he is feeling;

- integrate – manage his feelings and incorporate his traumatic experiences into his life story;

- adapt – develop new, adaptive responses and let go of maladaptive responses, recover social connectedness, self-esteem and the capacity for joy.

Sometimes the people around the child do not recognise that he has a post-traumatic disorder. Even if they do, they often don't understand what he needs or how best to manage his behaviour and address his problems. The best people to help a traumatised child are adults who know about the effects of traumatic life experience and can analyse the needs of traumatised children.

In this session, we will look at the three stages of recovery and what we can do to help.

SLIDE 24 **Stabilisation**

- **Safety**
  - **Children cannot begin to recover until they feel safe enough**
- **Learning about trauma**
  - **Victims of trauma need to gain understanding of their own responses**
- **Words for feelings**
  - **Getting the brain working to produce words for feelings makes it possible to process trauma**

Feeling safe involves both a safe physical environment and a safe "human" environment, i.e. with attachment figures whom the child trusts.

Traumatised children don't understand why they feel and behave the way they do. To make sense of it, they need to know about what happens to human beings when they are traumatised – someone needs to explain to them about the common human reaction to extreme threat and its long-term effects. The child's attachment figures can help to give her some insight into how this applies to her.

Trusted adults can help the child to get the "switched-off" parts of her brain functioning again. She needs to rediscover how to talk about her feelings and put a name to her confusion, fear, anger and pain. Expressing her inner experience will help her to process the trauma.

SLIDE 25   Enhancing a sense of safety

- Ensuring that every child has some space where they feel safe
- Learning how sensory experience increases the sense of safety for this child
- Experimenting with the space in discussion with the child
- Encouraging the child to generalise the feeling of safety through imagination

The child not only needs to *be* in a safe environment, but also needs to *feel* that he is in a safe environment.

Post-traumatic stress produces a generalised feeling of fear and anxiety. So however safe the environment is, if the child does not actually *feel* safe then his stress will continue. The challenge is to find a space where the child does feel safe. If he has a favourite place he retreats to, work out with him what it is about the space that makes it feel safe.

For instance, a child might come home from school every day and run straight up to his bedroom to hide under the bed. Try to work out with him why he likes it there. Is it the feeling of being in an enclosed, dark place? Being away from other people and the television? Being upstairs? Being in a place that no one else can enter?

Another child might feel safe only in a high-stimulus environment with other people around and the television on or loud music playing, and silence might make him feel anxious or afraid.

See if you can generalise the feeling of safety to other places. If a child only feels safe when he is in bed, would bringing his duvet downstairs and sitting wrapped up in it in a corner of the living room work as well?

 Question: Has any child you have cared for had a special place where he seemed to feel safe? Where was it and what was it like?

SLIDE 26   Helping children to regulate stress

- Traumatised children usually need help to develop or regain stress regulation
- This must involve learning how to recognise and change their own physiological state
- Learning to regulate arousal takes patience and practice

Children whose brain function has been affected by traumatic stress have lost – or never developed – the ability to regulate stress, so they usually need help to learn this or to re-learn it. They need to become aware of their own physiology and to notice their own reactions and responses, for instance, when they are becoming anxious or angry.

They also need to learn how to manage these reactions and responses and find ways to relax and calm themselves down. As well as help from their carers, this may require some specific treatments such as relaxation therapy or anger management training.

It will probably take a long time because traumatised children have developed a pattern of immediate response rather than responses based on thinking and self-control.

SLIDE 27 Teaching children about trauma

- Before children can start to engage they must begin to understand and recognise their own stress arousal
- To do this they need to learn about the effects of trauma
- Children can be helped to gain insight into their own stress responses

Children need to learn about stress, impulse, mood and the effects of trauma. Teenagers often tend to be interested in how their bodies function and this can be presented to them as part of health education.

Teaching traumatised children about the effects of traumatic stress on human beings will help them to understand that their own responses are ordinary reactions to extraordinary events. It gives them a cognitive model to use to make sense of their own out-of-control feelings.

They need to understand that they can develop some control over their own level of arousal and learn how to modulate their own responses. Help the child to gain some insight into the kind of things that affect her – for instance, is she more likely to lose her temper if she is tired or hungry?

SLIDE 28 Teaching words for feelings

- Notice non-verbal signals of feelings and help the child to recognise and name what is happening
- Start with powerful feelings
  - angry, sad, frightened
- Add in more subtle feelings
  - happy, lonely, sympathetic, awed

It is vital for traumatised children to develop emotional literacy. Whatever their state of emotional intelligence before being affected by trauma, they will undoubtedly need concentrated help with this afterwards.

 Question: When a child can't or won't tell you how she is feeling, what non-verbal signals might tell you instead?

A child might stomp around the house or damage things, she might twitch or shake, her skin colour might change or she might go rigid – these are all non-verbal signals of what is going on inside. You need to help the child to recognise and name her feelings so that in future she can learn to express how she feels by talking about it rather than "acting it out" in destructive ways.

SLIDE 29   Practising emotional literacy

- Be willing to demonstrate reflection on your own feelings
- Help the child to reflect on their feelings and apply their developing vocabulary
- Encourage them to think about what other people may be feeling
- Show the child that feelings change when expressed
- Help the child to realise the benefits of processing feelings through language

Children need to know that we adults are human beings with feelings too. Some traumatised children develop the belief that they – and they alone – are responsible for the feelings of the adults around them. We need to let them see that we do have feelings but that our feelings are not their responsibility.

Some children are extremely sensitive to even minor signals of irritation in the adults who care for them and will continuously ask: 'What's wrong?' With a child like this, it can be hard to be on the receiving end – some people say it feels as though he is 'all over you like a rash'!

Children can learn that feelings sometimes change when they are expressed. They can learn that telling someone how angry you are is sometimes preferable to going upstairs and smashing up your room.

SLIDE 30   Integration

- **Physiological self-management**
  - Children must be able to self-regulate in order to process trauma safely
- **Emotional processing**
  - Informal life-space interventions and formal therapy
- **Cognitive reconstruction**
  - Letting go of trauma-based thinking

The process of integration has three aspects:

- Traumatised children usually need help in developing or regaining the ability to regulate stress. This means learning how to recognise their own physiological state – whether they are anxious, afraid, angry, etc – and knowing how to change this. It takes patience and practice to learn to understand and calm down your own stress arousal.

- We need to build and extend the child's ability to use language to express her emotional experience. The ability to express her traumatic experience will eventually render it harmless and allow her to consign it to memory. There are many ways of helping a child through this process. Sometimes it will involve carers and others helping the child to express her feelings differently on a day-to-day basis; at other times or with other children it may involve more formal types of therapy.

- Children who have been traumatised develop beliefs and thoughts about themselves, their lives and the world that have been shaped by their experiences. They need to let go of this trauma-based thinking and develop new beliefs and assumptions that will help them to have a more positive view of themselves and the world.

SLIDE 31   Teaching children about relaxation

- Once children have some insight into their own responses they are ready to learn to gain some control of those responses
- Relaxation is a change in physiology
- Different approaches work for different people
- Relaxation may at first be painful for traumatised children hooked on stress hormones
- Everyone in the household can practise relaxation

Relaxation involves a change in the body's internal chemistry from being in a stressed state to being in a calm, pleasant state. Traumatised children are used to being in a state of arousal, a state of permanent "red alert". Having to do without this high arousal can almost be like "cold turkey" in an addict deprived of drugs. We need to teach children that although it may not be easy at first to learn to relax, relaxing will make them feel good.

(But be aware that there have been cases in which child abusers have first used relaxation exercises with the child in order to get him into a compliant state. For a child who has been subject to this or something similar, the idea and process of relaxation will feel even more threatening.)

It will help the child if you remember your own need to relax. When you are good to yourself, you are good to your child. Relaxation can be catching!

 Question: What kind of things do you do in your own life in order to relax?

Different things work for different people: sport, playing or listening to music, going to the pub with friends, snooker, cycling, walking, the outdoors, dancing, yoga, meditation, a scented bath . . .

SLIDE 32   Helping children to connect to their physical experience

- When children dissociate they cannot connect to their own experience
- They need help to recognise physical experiences such as hot/cold or sweet/sour
- Children cannot regulate arousal until they can recognise it

Give participants an example of dissociation: when someone has injured their foot badly and they have to get somewhere to save their life, they can somehow "dissociate" or cut off from the pain in order to get help. The pain doesn't kick in until you have got where you need to go.

Some traumatised children are dissociated or cut off from their own feelings – dissociation is when the sense of self "splits up" as a defensive measure against being overwhelmed by fear or horror. It keeps a part of your self unaffected by what is going on around you. The problem is that the brain learns to "cut off" from outside stimuli. Children remain in a dissociated state in which all their senses have been numbed – even feelings as basic as being too hot or too cold may have been affected.

These children need our help to get back in touch with their senses. Encourage the child to do activities that will help with this, such as kneading clay or bread dough, cooking, playing with wet cornflour, playing games that involve taste and smell ('Is that salt or is it sugar?'; 'Which scent do you like best?').

SLIDE 33   Practising relaxation techniques

- We need to learn the child – what works for this individual person to produce the relaxation response?
- Which senses are most involved?
  - *Sight*: lighting, colour, images
  - *Hearing*: rhythm, music, words, silence
  - *Smell*: relaxing oils, clothing, pets
  - *Taste*: milk, chocolate, special food, special drinks
  - *Touch*: fabric, water, massage

We are all different and, as we've just heard, we all have our own ways of relaxing. Try to work out what will help this particular child to relax. Approach this with a child or teenager as you would with a toddler and work out what kind of thing calms her down, settles her and helps her to sleep.

What senses are involved in helping us feel relaxed (or stressed)? Here are a few examples:

- The quality of light can play a role – artificial lighting can have a bad effect on particular children. Try using daylight lightbulbs to see if that makes a difference.

- Certain colours and colour schemes can also be more relaxing to the eye and affect our mood. Try using coloured lightbulbs.

- Looking out onto a vista, with the eyes in long focus, is relaxing. If your house is small and there is no long view from your windows, try hanging pictures with a vista instead, to give the experience of focusing on something far away.

- Hearing also plays a role. Listening to certain rhythms can slow down the heartbeat. Some children may be hypersensitive to sounds in their environment that others would not notice, such as a fridge humming. Some are made uncomfortable by silence.

- Be aware that certain smells, tastes and places might remind a child of a situation in which she was abused. For instance, being among trees might be relaxing for some children – but the opposite would, of course, be the case for any child who was abused in a wood. The smell of cigarette smoke or a particular aftershave might remind a child of an abuser.

SLIDE 34   Building and extending emotional experience

- Create spaces for feelings
  - quiet times with the child
  - special times of day/week
  - special settings
- Use every opportunity to extend emotional vocabulary
  - television programmes
  - books, plays, films
  - accounts the child gives of experience

You need to help the child get back in touch with his feelings. Ask him about what makes him feel safe and comforted; if he doesn't know, explore this with him.

For example, if the child is attached to you, taking a scarf or tissue with your scent on it to school with him might help. He can use it through the day to make him feel that you are close and to help him relax. Alternatively, if he is more attached to the family dog than to you, a bit of the dog blanket might be more effective!

Massage is not recommended with children who have been abused or traumatised, but you can teach the child self-massage. Some children find it almost impossible to be held or hugged but you may be able to find other opportunities to give a caring touch, such as hand care, foot care and hair care.

Stories, plays and art throughout the ages have been inspired by the experiences of human beings under extreme threat. By talking to the child you can help him connect to these themes and start to reflect on how his own experience has affected him. On another level, soap operas and films also provide opportunities to explore other people's feelings and relate them to the child's own experiences and reactions.

SLIDE 35   Making sense of the world

- There are three core assumptions essential for good mental health (Janoff-Bulman):
  - that the world is benevolent
  - that the world is meaningful
  - that we are worthy
- Traumatised children often cannot make sense of the world
- They may live with cognitive distortions
- They may suffer processing disorders

Ronnie Janoff-Bulman (1992) came up with a model for thinking about the impact that trauma has on our ability to think. He considers that human beings are able to maintain good mental health by having three basic assumptions about the world; that the world is good and kind, that our lives have meaning, and that we are worthy or deserving. These assumptions are a way that we explain the world to ourselves – patterns of thinking that are even more deep-seated than beliefs. They originate in babyhood when our brains are forming in response to the way we are nurtured by our parents or other attachment figures.

These assumptions actually have no basis in fact and our life experience often shows us that they are not the case – yet without these assumptions, we cannot function effectively.

Traumatic experience shatters these assumptions or prevents them from forming in the first place.

SLIDE 36   Examples of cognitive distortion

- Distorted beliefs about the self
  - Unattractiveness
  - Dangerousness
- Distorted beliefs about others
  - People who love me abuse me
  - Other people are dangerous
- Distorted beliefs about the world
  - Public services such as schools, hospitals, social services, are dangerous
  - Crime is normal

Children are still forming their sense of who they are and how they fit into the world. This is why they are particularly vulnerable to the effects of trauma. Trauma can take over the heart of their sense of identity.

The core assumptions that underlie the thinking of a traumatised child are quite different from those of others. She perceives the world as a dangerous and inhospitable place and other people as likely to reject her or hurt her.

The dynamics of trauma involve a descending spiral of helplessness, hopelessness and the loss of all sense of positive identity and self-worth.

SLIDE 37 Examples of processing disorders

- **Visual processing**
  - **Enhanced peripheral vision = distractibility**
  - **Diminished focused vision = poor concentration on visual tasks**
- **Auditory processing**
  - **Filtering for danger = loss of hearing for human voice**
  - **Not hearing the beginning, ending, or significant words in any sentence = poor comprehension**
  - **Inability to process negative commands leading to false assessment on compliance-defiance axis**

Apart from distortions in thinking, a traumatised child may suffer from distortions in perception too.

The effect of trauma on the brain may result in disorders in the way the child perceives things visually. If he has difficulty in focusing, this can make it hard to concentrate on what is in front of him. Being more tuned in to things on the periphery of his vision than things in the centre can mean he is easily distracted.

In terms of his hearing, he may be more tuned in to background sounds because he is alert for signs of danger. This can make it harder to hear and concentrate on the voice of the person who is speaking. He may also miss certain parts of what is said to him. And if a child fails to hear when he is told not to do something, he is quite likely to do it – which means the adults around him perceive him as disobedient and defiant.

 Question: Does this sound familiar when you think about children you have cared for?

SLIDE 38 Helping children to let go of cognitive distortions

- **Trauma takes over core identity – traumatic identity**
- **Direct challenge to distorted thinking will usually be rejected**
- **We need to create alternatives that work for the child**
  - *For example*: **'Everyone who loves me abuses me'**
    - **Can you think of one person who loves you and has not abused you?**
    - **How would you know someone loved you if they did not abuse you?**
- **Such work must take account of any processing disorders: what sense does the child make of our ideas?**

The different core assumptions, or "cognitive schemas", produce what is known as "traumatic identity" – an identity and personality shaped by the traumatic experience. We cannot change such core assumptions simply by contradicting them – if you try to reason with the child and persuade her that her view of the world is mistaken, you will find that she is impervious to logic.

The way to change cognitive schemas is by *adding* new ones, not trying to take away the existing ones. With time and patience we can help a child to develop alternative schemas. We need to generate more positive assumptions by helping the child think through them and develop them for herself, rather than by telling her directly that her world view is wrong.

At first, these new schemas will co-exist alongside the traumatic schemas, even though they contradict each other. But eventually the child may adopt the new schemas and let go of the old ones.

Exercise: How can we help a child to develop new and more positive assumptions?

Ask the participants to divide into small groups. Ask each group to suggest ways of helping a child develop more positive assumptions as alternatives to the following traumatic schema below (write these on the flip chart). The groups should try to come up with at least three ways they might try to challenge each traumatic schema in conversation and day-to-day life with the child. They should write their suggestions down. After 30 minutes' discussion, ask each group to feed their ideas back to the rest of the participants.

- 'People who love me abuse me.'

- 'Everything I do goes wrong.'

- 'Everybody I care about abandons me.'

- 'I am ugly and repulsive.'

- 'People who care for me become ill and die.'

- 'I do not deserve to be happy and if I am happy something bad will happen.'

Taking the schema 'I am ugly and repulsive' as an example, one way of helping the child develop a new assumption might be to find one feature (hands, nails, hair) that the child can accept may be attractive and help the child to take extra care of that feature. Another way would be to encourage the child to take part in physical activities that build positive body awareness such as dance, martial arts and gymnastics. Another way would be to talk about role models in the child's world – what is it that makes people attractive to others?

In the case of the last schema, 'I do not deserve to be happy and if I am happy something bad will happen', one way to generate alternative possibilities for the child might include starting a conversation about the way in which traumatised people tend to notice only the bad things, not the good ones. Remind the child of some positive experiences to bring these into his conscious awareness. Another way would be to identify an occasion when the child has been happy and has stayed safe.

SLIDE 39　Adaptation

- **Re-establishing social connectedness**
  - Encouraging the development of a variety of social relationships
- **Building self-esteem**
  - Promoting self-esteem through a range of interactions and activities
- **Developing the capacity for joy**
  - Actively encouraging the child to recognise, name and remember experiences of pleasure and wonder

After integration comes adaptation. After trauma, we are different people. Our personality will have changed forever. Once the child has integrated her experience into her life story and let go of trauma-based thinking, she needs to adapt to the new, changed person that she is now. She needs to develop new, adaptive responses and let go of her old ways of responding.

Successful adaptation means re-establishing social relationships with other people, building self-esteem and learning how to enjoy life and experience pleasure and happiness.

SLIDE 40　Encouraging social connectedness

- Promoting reflection and awareness of social presentation
- Teaching social skills
- Informal life-space work and formal planned and structured interventions
- Individual and group work
  - School or college
  - Family and care setting
  - Community groups

Human beings are social animals and by far the most significant things in our world are other human beings.

Traumatised children lose the ability to understand or take pleasure in social relationships. Carers need to help them recover a sense of being connected to other people and to think about their relationships with friends, family, teachers and so on. Family gatherings, school or college activities, emotional literacy activities such as circle time, and sports and clubs such as Scouts, music and dance classes can all help children to develop their social skills and build their self-esteem. For some children, more formal intervention might be needed too.

SLIDE 41   Building self-esteem

- Integrated approach across all settings
  - Home
  - School
  - Community groups
- Adults need to be aware of the vulnerability of traumatised children to shame and criticism
- Self-esteem work begins where the child is: what do they value about themselves?
- It also opens the door to new self-knowledge: the positive perceptions of others
- It must be put into words

Once a child has achieved some measure of stability and integration – but not before – activities to improve her self-esteem can begin. This is a vital step towards recovery from trauma. Ideally, all the adults involved with the child, in whatever setting, will be aware of the need to build her self-esteem. Sometimes, teachers see only the defiant and disruptive teenager – as carers we should try to help them see the frightened and shamed child inside.

We need to recognise and praise every small achievement, everything the child does that is positive – in school, in the community and at home. For a child who has been neglected or abused, the experience of being praised, rewarded and valued by other people will be completely new.

SLIDE 42   Developing the capacity for joy

- Encourage existing and new activities
  - Individual and shared
  - Low stimulus and high stimulus
- Experiment with different words to attach to different experiences of joy
  - Pleasure
  - Happiness
  - Wonder
  - Awe
  - And so on
- Practise remembering feeling happy

Trauma robs us of the capacity to experience joy. In most people, when they experience pleasure – anything from simple enjoyment to complete bliss – this is accompanied by physical signs, such as particular patterns of electrical activity in the brain and the release of hormones called endorphins. When someone is traumatised, the brain loses this function. We need to help the traumatised child to recapture this ability to feel delight and joy.

The capacity to experience joy is vital if we are to live our lives to the full. Until a child has this, our work of helping him to recover is not complete. How do we do it? We have to provide access to potentially joyful experiences and encourage the child to become aware of feelings of wonder, delight and pleasure. We need to help him remember those times when he did feel happy, because they will help him through the more mundane times.

As carers, we ourselves need to be able to experience joy. If we cannot feel it ourselves, we will not be able to help a child to experience it.

Question: What kind of thing gives you feelings of wonder, awe, delight and joy? Can you think of some examples of activities, places and experiences that might produce those same feelings in a child?

SLIDE 43   UN Convention on the Rights of the Child

- **Article 39 says that 'States parties' (this includes the UK):**
- **. . . shall take all appropriate measures to promote the physical and psychological recovery and social reintegration of a child victim of:**
  - **any form of neglect, exploitation, or abuse**
  - **torture or any other form of cruel, inhuman or degrading treatment or punishment**
  - **armed conflicts**
- **Such recovery and reintegration shall take place in an environment which fosters the health, self-respect and dignity of the child**

The United Nations (UN) is an organisation that has considerable expertise in understanding and treating trauma.

Article 39 of the UN Convention on the Rights of the Child sets the standard internationally for the treatment of traumatised children. It states that all appropriate measures should be taken to promote the child's physical and psychological recovery and social reintegration, and that this should be done in an environment which fosters the child's health, self-respect and dignity. This is exactly what you are doing when you work with a traumatised child in the way you have learned about today.

Article

About trauma

This article is extracted from Working with Traumatised Children
Level 4 BTEC Qualification available online from Akamas
(Also available on the CD-ROM)

Trauma and traumatic stress

Trauma means injury. In general usage, when we talk about trauma we mean a traumatic event. This is defined in the *Diagnostic and Statistical Manual of Mental Disorders* (APA, 1994) as:

- an event that involves actual or threatened death or serious injury, or other threat to one's personal integrity;

  OR

- witnessing an event that involves death, injury, or a threat to the physical integrity of another person;

  OR

- learning about unexpected or violent death, serious harm, or threat of death or injury experienced by a family member or other close associate;

  AND

- the person's response to the event must involve intense fear, helplessness or horror;

  OR

- in children, the response must involve disorganised or agitated behaviour.

  When human beings experience such terrible events our usual stability is overwhelmed. Our day-to-day survival depends on being able to think and plan. In extreme conditions this is too slow to save us. The human body responds to traumatic events by instantly producing massive amounts of hormones that switch off our usual functions and switch on extreme survival functions. We stop thinking and start acting on primitive impulses.

  In order to stop thinking, blood flow changes in the brain, with some areas being deprived of blood supply. In order to start acting, blood flow changes in the body, with some areas being deprived of blood supply and other areas getting extra blood. This automatic response to terror is called traumatic stress. It is traumatic, that is, it involves injury, because loss of blood supply injures the brain and changed blood supply injures the body.

  In order to survive extreme threat we suffer traumatic stress. Survival injures us.

Traumatic stress and brain function: Day to day experience, repeated throughout waking hours (Adapted from van der Kolk *et al*, 1996, p 294)

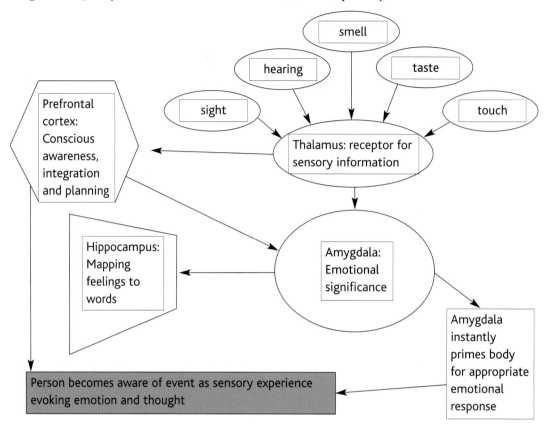

What happens when we are exposed to trauma?

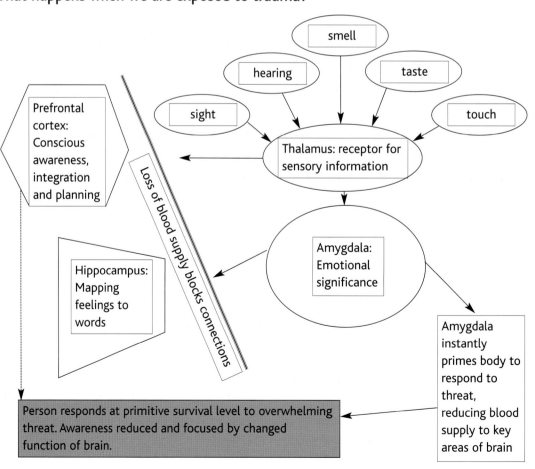

Experience of traumatic events

We experience the world through our sensory organs. Every waking moment our senses are working, informing our conscious and unconscious experience of the world.

The following process happens many times a day and takes a tiny fraction of a second.

- Sensory information travels as raw data to an area of the limbic (primitive, unconscious) brain called the thalamus, where it begins to be processed so that we can become aware that something has happened.

- The thalamus splits the signal and sends information in two directions:
  - to the prefrontal cortex
  - and to another area of the limbic brain called the amygdala. The amygdala is that area of the brain that attaches emotional significance to our experience.

- The information arriving at the prefrontal cortex is in turn transmitted from there to the amygdala, so that information arrives at the amygdala from two directions.

- The signal arriving from the prefrontal cortex is evaluated for emotional significance.

- Information about the emotional significance of the experience is returned to the cortex by way of the hippocampus, another limbic brain structure that, among many functions, allows us to put words to feelings.

- Now the prefrontal cortex has assembled a fully evaluated sensory experience.

- **Only what is happening in the prefrontal cortex is available to us as conscious experience.**

BUT

- The information passed from the thalamus direct to the amygdala travels faster than the information from the prefrontal cortex.

- This direct information is instantly evaluated by the amygdala for emotional significance.

- The evaluation is passed on to areas in the primitive brainstem that control hormonal responses.

- Sensory information evaluated as extreme threat causes the hormonal response known as traumatic stress.

- This closes down the function of the prefrontal cortex before it can assemble and process the sensory information it has received.

- **We cannot think about traumatic events while they are happening.**

For example:

- A parent hears a child cry.

- The sound is transmitted from the ear as sensory information to the thalamus.

- The signal is split:
  - The amygdala evaluates the emotional impact of the cry and provokes a hormone response priming the parent to respond.
  - The prefrontal cortex receives the information and transmits a signal to the amygdala to evaluate the emotional content of the cry.
  - The hippocampus receives information from the amygdala and transmits the information to the prefrontal cortex.

- The parent recognises that the child is crying and thinks about how to respond to the cry.

OR

- A parent hears a child scream in terror.

- The sound is transmitted from the ear as sensory information to the thalamus.

- The signal is split:
  - The amygdala evaluates the emotional impact of the scream and provokes a hormone response of traumatic stress.
  - Areas of the prefrontal cortex close down.

- The parent leaps into action to save the child without stopping to think.

Spontaneous recovery from traumatic stress

Most people, most of the time, recover spontaneously from traumatic stress.

In order to recover we need three things:

- safety;

- a supportive social network with secure attachment relationships;

- the ability to express what has happened.

Human memory is generally linked to the story of our lives, the narrative we relate to ourselves and others about who we are and how we are. Such memory relies on the functioning of our conscious mind, which in turn relies on the functioning of our prefrontal cortex.

Ordinary memory does not work after trauma, because the parts of the brain that deal with memory do not work. Instead there is a record of the traumatic event held in the amygdala, which ordinarily serves to evaluate the emotional significance of any sensory information. Highly emotionally charged sensory experience imprints itself in the amygdala. This is an unstable situation. To reach equilibrium and stability, the brain will need to discharge and process this information.

The process of recovery is not a straight line but is more like a spiral. It has three phases that repeat until the whole experience is processed and the traumatic event has become a memory of an experience that changed us but did not destroy us.

- **Stabilisation (avoidance)**
  - The body registers that the threat is over but we are still unable to think about the trauma and will avoid anything that reminds us of the event.
  - We establish that the network around us is safe and trustworthy.
  - Stress levels begin to drop.
  - We begin to recover the ability to think.

- **Integration (intrusion)**
  - Flashback: the amygdala discharges a fragment of stored traumatic experience.
  - Stress levels rise but our trusted attachment figures (friends and family) help us to feel safe and we do not become overwhelmed.
  - We tell the story of that bit of our experience, processing the terror through language, or children will at this point of recovery re-enact an aspect of the trauma through play.
  - Our attachment figures help us to think about what happened and put it into the story of our lives.

- **Adaptation**
  - Thinking about the traumatic event allows us to take stock of our lives and notice how our world has changed.
  - We get a sense of how we can live with the changes in our lives.
  - We begin to imagine life after recovery.

- **Stabilisation (avoidance)**
  - Stress levels have risen in recalling aspects of the trauma.
  - There is a period of avoidance, when we cannot think about anything to do with the trauma.
  - Stress levels fall again.

- **Integration (intrusion)**
  - Flashback: the amygdala discharges a fragment of stored traumatic experience.
- And so on, until the whole experience has been processed and the traumatic event has become part of our life story that we can recount to ourselves or others without becoming overwhelmed and retraumatised by the memory.

2 Resilience

Understanding resilience after trauma

This is the first session of the second part of the course, so welcome the participants and put them at their ease.

Explain what they can expect from the course – that there will be some direct input from you, in terms of your slide presentation, but that they also have a lot to contribute from their own knowledge and experience. Explain that they will not simply be sitting and listening to you – they will be actively involved in discussion and group exercises, coming up with their own thoughts, ideas and suggestions.

Introductions

If any participants are new to the group and did not attend earlier sessions, ask participants to introduce themselves to the rest of the group.

Ground rules

You may want to reiterate the ground rules that were set out at the start of Session A in Part 1 of this course – *Trauma*.

Provide the handout

Give participants a handout of the slide presentation so that they do not need to write everything down – they can make additional notes on their handout if this is helpful.

SLIDE 1   Learning outcomes

- To understand "resilience" in relation to recovery from childhood trauma
- To understand resilience in the context of the child's various social networks
- To identify factors that contribute to resilience and people who can help
- To plan ways of building on the child's strengths and increasing resilience

This slide shows the learning outcomes for Sessions A and B, *Understanding resilience after trauma*.

SLIDE 2   Transitions, resilience and human ecology

Transitions are life events and changes. We don't go through life in a straight line – there are distinct points at which our lives change and we change. None of us can go through life without any transitions.

Some people are more affected by transitions than others. The same is true of children who have been traumatised.

In this session we will look at transitions and resilience – the ability to survive and thrive when life gets tough. We will also look at the different areas of a child's life where you can support and build on her strengths as a way of increasing her resilience.

SLIDE 3 About transitions

- Life stages that change us, such as:
  - Walking
  - Talking
  - Puberty
  - Becoming sexually active
  - Becoming an adult
  - Mid-life
  - Old age

Some life stages, listed on this slide, are a general part of human development – they are universal and happen wherever and however people live.

SLIDE 4 Socially determined transitions

- Different in different societies and social groups, such as:
  - Going to school
  - Leaving school
  - Further/higher education
  - Entering employment
  - Retirement

These transitions are socially determined – children have to go to school and adults have to work and then eventually retire. The ages at which they occur and the implications will differ depending on factors such as your social group and the country you live in.

SLIDE 5 Culturally determined transitions

- Different in different cultural groups, such as:
  - Religious conversion
  - Initiation into a religious community
  - Initiation into adult life
  - Marriage
  - Parenthood
  - Old age

These are culturally determined transitions. "Becoming an adult" can take very different forms, for instance, in some societies initiation into adulthood may be surrounded by certain rites of passage in which young people have to prove their bravery or strength. In our society, although the age at which young people become adults in the eyes of the law is 18, transition to adulthood is seen as a more gradual process as the young person becomes independent, including financially independent.

SLIDE 6 Transitions arising from individual circumstances

- Some transitions are individual and personal:
  - Moving house
  - Forming a new household
  - Having a child
  - Becoming unemployed
  - Having a serious illness or accident
  - Becoming disabled
  - Being involved in a disaster

Some transitions do not happen to everyone. They may be planned or expected, or they may occur out of the blue. There are some transitions that we choose and we plan and work towards, such as moving house and getting a new job. Others are unwelcome, such as disability or being involved in a disaster. Some transitions may turn out to be short-lived – we may lose our job, for example, but be unemployed for only a short time until we find another. Other transitions have lifelong implications, such as having a child.

SLIDE 7 Transitions and traumatised children

- All transitions are stressful
- Developmental trauma – never having developed stress regulation
- Emotional trauma – impaired ability to regulate stress
- Without stress regulation all transitions may be traumatic

Even if we wanted the transition and chose it and welcomed it, every transition involves some stress. We have to adapt to the new situation and we have to take on board what we have gained or lost. This causes stress and has implications for children who have been traumatised.

If a baby's attachment needs are not met, if he does not have a carer who is reliable and attuned to him and he does not develop a sense of safety, he will not develop the ability to regulate stress. His brain function will be compromised. This is *developmental trauma*.

Some children develop the ability to regulate stress in babyhood but then, at a stage when they are able to process their feelings, are exposed to terrifying events. Overwhelming fear or horror leads to extreme stress, which can injure the brain and impair the child's ability to regulate stress from then on. This is emotional trauma.

Children who are not able to regulate stress effectively find stressful experiences difficult to manage.

All transitions are stressful – so, for these children, transitions are particularly difficult and perhaps even traumatic.

SLIDE 8   About resilience

- The ability to survive and thrive under difficult conditions
  - Resilient people continue to develop to their own potential even when circumstances are against them
- Different from coping
  - Survive but at cost to own healthy development
- Individual and social factors contribute

Different people have different abilities to manage transitions, and one individual may have the ability to manage one particular transition better than others. The key to understanding these differences is the idea of resilience.

Resilience is not the same as coping. When we cope with difficulties we survive them, but at the cost of our own healthy development – for instance, we may use alcohol as a crutch, become depressed, avoid certain situations or vent our feelings on others in inappropriate ways. When we are resilient, we find ways of dealing with change that allow us to continue to develop to our full potential.

What makes us more or less resilient? Some of the factors are to do with us as individuals, others are to do with social factors such as the amount of support we have from family, friends and the wider community.

All of us, all the time, are both resilient and vulnerable. And our resilience and vulnerability are changing all the time – affected by circumstances and events, dented by ill-health or boosted by a holiday or fun night out with friends.

Of course, some events are so traumatic that anyone, however resilient, would be harmed by them. And some people are so vulnerable that most transition events will harm them.

Many traumatised children are remarkably resilient. They seem able to bounce back even from terrible events and thrive in a secure and nurturing environment. Others, of course, do not. But all children, however great the adversity they have survived, can be helped to adapt and increase their resilience.

SLIDE 9   The ecology of human development

- People develop within a network of relationships:
  - The individual and immediate attachment figures
  - Family and kinship groups
  - Significant others
  - The wider community
- Resilience factors occur at all these levels

This slide shows something called "the ecology of human development", a term developed by Urie Bronfenbrenner and the title of a book he wrote in 1979.

We are all part of a social system and live our lives within a network of relationships. These relationships occur at different levels or layers.

- The closest are our immediate attachment figures – for a child, this is the primary carer or carers. The child and primary carer or carers form the core group. This core may be contained within a household and live with other members of the family.

- Then at the next layer there are other important people who play a direct part in the child's life – these may include her birth parents and siblings whom she no longer lives with but has contact with; teachers; therapists; close friends.

- A further layer is the wider community, involving other pupils and teachers at school, health care workers, neighbours, shop assistants she sees regularly and so on.

- There is a further ecological layer consisting of people whom the child does not have contact with, but whose actions and decisions can affect her because they affect the institutions she relies on – such as school governors, hospital managers, local councillors and so on.

- Finally, all the ecological layers are held within a social order which determines the nature and type of organisations and relationships that can exist. For instance, is the child living in a stable and democratic society or one in which civil society is breaking down and lawlessness is rife?

  All of these levels affect people's resilience.

SLIDE 10   Resilience and transitions

- **Think of a transition in your own life which you worked through successfully**
    - **What happened?**
    - **What did you lose as a result?**
    - **What did you gain?**
    - **What helped you come through successfully?**
    - **What do you think is the link between resilience and successful transitions?**

Exercise

Ask participants to work in pairs (preferably with someone they do not already know well). Ask them to discuss, with their partner, the questions on Slide 10. Allow them around 15 minutes to talk to each other about transitions they have experienced and what kind of things helped them at the time. The transitions they choose should be ones that they worked through successfully and that were long enough ago for them to be able to look at the short and long-term effects.

Then ask each pair to feed back their ideas about what made them able to manage the transitions successfully. Write up their points on the flipchart. Encourage participants to discuss their own experiences and the kind of qualities and support that enabled them to come through. Encourage the group to see the common themes emerging.

It is likely that most of these points will relate to resilience factors which help people to get through tough times and make successful transitions. You will be covering these in more detail later in the presentation.

SLIDE 11   The transition to adult life

- Make a list of key knowledge and skills needed to survive and thrive as an adult, such as:
  - Legal knowledge
  - Financial knowledge
  - Medical knowledge
  - Home maintenance skills
  - Driving/cycling/using public transport
  - And so on
- How many of these did you already understand or know how to do when you became an adult?

This slide shows some of the knowledge needed to negotiate adult life successfully. Ask participants to call out other suggestions, while you write them down on the flipchart.

Young people have to make the transition to adulthood. Point out how much a young person still has to learn before she becomes an effectively functioning and independent adult, able to solve most of the challenges of day-to-day life.

SLIDE 12   Resilience is the key to successful transitions

- People manage transitions because:
  - They have previous experience of successful transitions
  - They believe in their own efficacy
  - They can tolerate stress
  - They have a problem-solving approach
  - They know how to get help from others
  - They have support from family and friends
  - They survive and thrive because they are resilient
  - Promoting resilience is the most effective way to prepare children and young people for the transition to adult care.

Refer back to the points you wrote on the flipchart, which participants said had helped them to come successfully through transitions. Some of these may echo the points made on this slide. We need to bear these things in mind when trying to increase children's resilience.

SLIDE 13   The six domains of resilience in childhood

- Factors increasing resilience can be organised into six domains (Daniel and Wassell, 2002)
  - Secure base
  - Education
  - Friendships
  - Talents and interests
  - Positive values
  - Social competencies

Brigid Daniel and Sally Wassell have written about assessing and promoting resilience in vulnerable children and adolescents. They identified six areas or "domains" which all have an impact on a child's resilience.

Those of you who are familiar with the seven dimensions of child development identified for the Looking After Children (LAC) System will see similarities with these domains. The LAC System was based on criteria for assessing the outcomes of parenting, while the domains of resilience are based on the factors that contribute to children's ability to survive and thrive in difficult circumstances.

SLIDE 14   Assessing resilience: secure base

- **The child has a sense of security**
- **There is a stable attachment relationship with carers**
- **Significant others are stable figures in the life of the child**
- **The wider community is stable and supportive**

The most important of all of these domains is the secure base. For a child, this is about his attachment figures, the key relationships in his day-to-day life, and his home or care setting.

The strength and security of his attachment relationships makes him more resilient. Losses in his secure base will make him much more vulnerable. Although all the domains contribute to resilience, the others have a less immediate and significant impact.

SLIDE 15   Assessing resilience: education

- **The child is doing well in school**
- **Carers support the child's education**
- **Significant others support and contribute to the child's education**
- **There is good local educational provision to meet the child's needs**

Some children may be resilient in some areas of their lives but barely cope in others. They may, for example, be doing well at school but be unable to manage the close relationships in the family. Or they may get on well at home but be quite unable to manage the demands of school life. Sometimes their impairments make the demands of school life particularly challenging.

SLIDE 16   Assessing resilience: friendships

- **The child understands friendship and can make and keep friends**
- **Carers support the child's friendships**
- **Significant others support the child's friendships**
- **There are opportunities in the wider community for the child to make friends**

Friendships can be a challenge for children who have been traumatised. In some cases, their volatility, need to control and lack of emotional empathy can make other children wary of them. They may be victimised, bullied or marginalised, or they themselves may do the bullying.

Traumatised children often recognise and seek out other children who have also suffered trauma.

Children who cannot manage their anger can even sometimes become the "loaded gun" of the school playground, exploited by others because of the ease with which they can be provoked to react.

Question: When you think about a particular child, does this sound familiar? How can you support the child in finding and keeping appropriate friendships?

SLIDE 17   Assessing resilience: talents and interests

- The child has talents and interests
- Carers support the child's talents and interests
- Significant others support and contribute to the child's talents and interests
- There are opportunities locally for the child to develop talents and interests

Talents and interests build self-esteem. Illustrate this by telling participants the true story of Donna, aged nine, who was placed in a foster family after many years of undetected abuse and neglect. In her foster home her behaviour was quite difficult but she loved going to school and began to do well there. The school had a brass band, which Donna joined. She discovered she had a talent for playing brass instruments. Soon she was invited to join a local brass band. Her carers tracked down a special bursary fund for gifted children and used the money to buy Donna her own trumpet. Donna's talent brought her friends, a social life and increased self-esteem. It increased her resilience.

 Question: Do you enjoy pursuing interests and talents of your own, or do you neglect your own talents and interests because you can't be bothered or are too busy looking after everyone else?

When participants have shared their thoughts about this, remind them that as carers they are role models for the children they look after. Making time to enjoy their own talents and hobbies sets a good example, as well as being good for them as individuals!

SLIDE 18   Assessing resilience: positive values

- The child understands feelings and shows age-appropriate moral reasoning
- Carers support and promote emotional literacy and moral reasoning
- Significant others support the development of positive values
- The wider community promotes positive values

Children with positive values are more resilient. Moral reasoning normally changes as the child develops through a series of moral stages.

Some children grow up in families where moral reasoning is simply unknown or is distorted – different "rules" apply and crime is seen as the norm. There may even be family members who actively discourage the child from developing positive values.

 Question: Have you looked after or worked with a child whose moral values were very different from your own family's? How did you handle this?

SLIDE 19 About positive values

- Age-appropriate capacity to:
  - Help others
  - Comfort others
  - Share with others
  - Understand the perspective of others
  - Apply moral reasoning

The best environment for a child to grow up in is one where the adults around him present and promote positive values such as caring, sharing and helping other people. They help him to understand what is acceptable social behaviour and try to help him develop empathy and moral reasoning.

SLIDE 20 Development of moral reasoning

- Developmental pathway
  Preconventional morality
  Focus on punishment
  Focus on reward
  Conventional morality
  Focus on relationships
  Focus on social order
  Postconventional morality
  Focus on rights
  Focus on truth and justice

There is a theory, Kohlberg's Universal Stage Model (Daniel and Wassell, 2002c) which sets out the moral stages children go through as they develop.

Preconventional morality:
- Young children begin to grasp the concept of actions having consequences. They do not understand rules, but believe that what is right is what their carers allow them to do, and what is wrong is what their carers do not allow them to do. Their focus is on punishment.

- If their needs are being met and they are developing healthily, they begin to apply a judgment about their own interests. They begin to recognise rules and will follow them if it will immediately benefit them. Their focus now is on reward.

Conventional morality:
- In middle childhood, many children develop a moral sense based on living up to other people's expectations of them. They value qualities that support group solidarity, such as loyalty. Their focus is on relationships.

- They may then develop to the next stage, of recognising that social rules and promises are important and should be kept. Their focus is on social order.

Postconventional morality:

- Some young people go on to develop moral reasoning based on an understanding that rules are relative to a group and that human rights should take precedence. Their focus is on rights.

- A few develop moral reasoning based on universal ethical principles – their focus is on truth and justice.

People who suffer trauma or adversity may regress to an earlier stage of moral reasoning. For example, we may have strong principles but under certain pressures we can become egocentric or rigid and rule-dominated.

SLIDE 21   Assessing resilience: social competencies

- **The child shows appropriate autonomy and self-belief**
- **Carers promote the social competence of the child**
- **Significant others support the development of social competence**
- **The wider community provides opportunities for the child to practise social competence**

For a child, having a sense of social competence enhances her resilience. There are many aspects to social competence – basically, it means being able to function well in a social context. It includes basic skills like looking after her own personal hygiene, travelling by public transport and using the telephone. Carers and others can nurture this ability by allowing the child some autonomy and encouraging her to do things for herself.

They can also find opportunities to allow her to practise social competence outside the home. Groups such as Brownies or Scouts provide opportunities to socialise, learn new skills and test oneself within a safe and supportive setting.

 Question: What ways can you think of to increase a child's social competence?

SLIDE 22   About social competencies

- **A broad area, which in terms of building resilience would include:**
  Autonomy
  Able and willing to take responsibility for self
  Self-control
  Able to control and regulate own behaviour
  Self-efficacy
  Believing in own ability to be effective in the world
  Attention
  Able to concentrate and focus on tasks and people

There are lots of way you can build a child's social competence in the areas of autonomy, self-control, self-efficacy and attention. For instance:

- Encourage him to take responsibility for himself

- Model self-control in your own behaviour and help him to develop self-control

- Praise him when he has managed to do something well, such as a school project or arranging a trip with friends

- Provide a room in the house in which he will be able to concentrate and encourage him to focus and pay attention when you are talking to him. Praise him when he has concentrated on something, such as a story or piece of homework.

2 Resilience

Building on strengths in the child and the social network

Provide each participant with a copy of the resilience map (see below) and green, amber and red pencils or crayons. (This map, and a completed example of the map, are also available on the CD-ROM.)

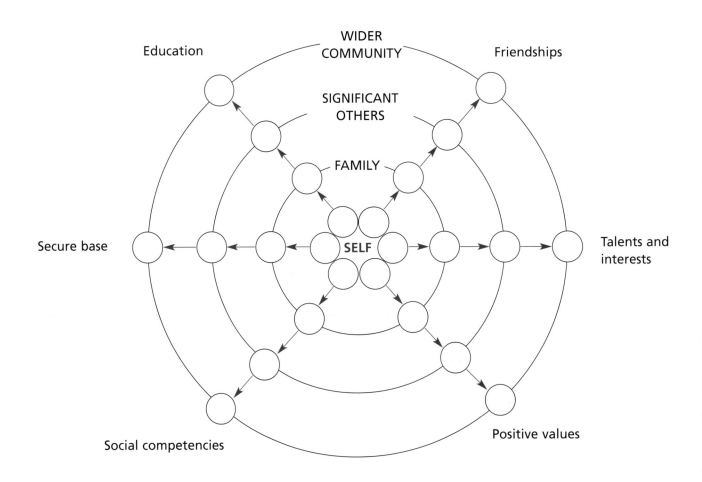

●●●●●●●●●●
SLIDE 23   Assessing resilience and making plans

In the previous session we learned what resilience is and why it matters.

In this session we will find out how we can map an individual child's resilience in the various domains and come up with a plan to work with the child or young person and others to increase resilience.

SLIDE 24   Working with the child or young person

- Working on resilience is the most effective preparation for the transition to adult life
- Such preparation takes place throughout childhood as resilience develops
- It is essential when working on resilience to work closely with the child or young person
- Assessing resilience is an intervention which in itself can contribute to preparing for transitions

We saw in the previous session that if someone has lots of personal strengths, a supportive family and friends and is well integrated into the community, he or she is more likely to be able to survive difficult circumstances. For a child, it means a better chance of a successful transition to adult life.

Resilience develops throughout childhood, so building resilience in children will help them in the years to come.

Explain to participants that in this session they will be mapping resilience in a child or young person. This is not a formal assessment of any kind, but an exercise to start on here and continue at home with the child or young person, if possible. It is important to work closely with the child or young person.

Explain that just doing the mapping exercise, in itself, will help. It will get the carer and the child to start thinking about resilience and how they can make small changes in the child's life that will contribute to building resilience.

SLIDE 25   A child in mind

- Think of a traumatised child or young person known to you
- Use the resilience map to build up a picture of the current state of resilience of this child or young person
- As you complete the map, consider how you could transfer this exercise to direct work with the child or young person

Ask participants to think about a child or young person they know who is adopted or in foster care or residential care. If they are currently fostering a child, they should do this exercise in relation to that child.

They will be using the resilience chart provided to help them form an assessment of the child's resilience in each domain. They will also look at ways they could apply their ideas in direct work with the child or young person. They will end up with a strategic plan to increase the child or young person's resilience and reduce their vulnerability.

SLIDE 26   Planning for the next transition

- Resilience maps can be used to help children and young people prepare for the next transition in their lives, and for the transition to adult life
- Once they have assessed and mapped their current state of resilience, they can use the map to think about areas at any ecological level where they have more or less resilience
- They can also develop ideas about
  WHAT will enable them to build the resilience they need
  WHO can help them with this

Tell participants the following:

Children and young people themselves can get a lot of benefit from completing a resilience chart for themselves. You will not, of course, be able to involve the child or young person in this today but you might like to explain it to him when you get home. The child or young person could complete the same exercise and map their own state of resilience or vulnerability in the different areas of their life. You can use this as the basis for talking to the child or young person about what and who might be able to help them.

SLIDE 27   Working with the support network

- Preparation for adult life for traumatised children cannot be achieved by working with the child alone
- Factors that contribute to resilience occur at every ecological level
- Systemic working is essential:
  The care setting
  Significant others in contact with the child
  The wider community
- Interventions at these levels can ensure that the young person will be able to manage the transition

One carer working alone with a child cannot do everything that the child needs in order to prepare for adult life. The factors that build a child's resilience are influenced by people and decisions at many different levels, from her foster carers to the policies of the agency, the education authority, the local authority and the health trust.

People in the care setting – such as foster carers and residential care workers – need to work with others who are significant in the child's life, such as birth parents, teachers and therapists.

The wider community also has a part to play and, wherever possible, children and their carers should engage at this level to make their voices heard, educate decision-makers, influence policy and lobby for improvements.

● ● ● ● ● ● ● ● ● ●

SLIDE 28   The support network for the child in mind

- Who are the key people who constitute the first layers of the support network for the child or young person you have been thinking about?
  - Foster carers or residential staff?
  - Family members?
  - Friends?
  - School staff?
  - Social worker?
  - Therapist?
  - Community activity leaders?
  - Religious community leaders?

Before participants start the exercise, ask them to think about the child or young person and the key people in his life at the first two layers of the support network. Some possible key people are shown on this slide. Ask them to write two lists, showing the people who are "carers" and "significant others" in the child's life.

Exercise

This exercise will take a lot of thought and will take up much of the session. While participants look at the resilience chart, talk them through the following:

Using this chart, please indicate your estimation of the resilience of the child in each domain and at each ecological level by using a simple green/amber/red code. If, in your opinion, the child is **resilient**, colour that segment **green**; if he is **coping**, colour the segment **amber**; if he is **vulnerable** in that domain and at that level, colour the segment **red**.

For example, in the domain of "secure base", do you think the child is resilient, coping or vulnerable? If you think the child or young person is vulnerable in their own sense of a secure base, you would colour the "child" segment in red.

At the level of "significant others", the child may have a close friend who has moved away, making them more vulnerable – but they may also have an adult sister who is supportive, a teacher they like and trust and a therapist who is helping them make progress with anger management. So on balance you might decide to colour the "significant others" segment green.

Here are some of the points you might consider when looking at the "secure base" domain:

Child: what is the evidence that the child feels secure or insecure?

- How does the child react to stress?

- Does he seek help if he is feeling stressed? From whom?

- Does he try to control other people?

- Does he seem confident that he will have the attention of adults when he needs it?

Carers: what is the evidence that the people caring for the child provide a secure base (if you yourself are the carer, try to reflect on the care you provide as though you were an outsider)

- Are the carers able to show commitment to the child?

- Does the environment meet the child's needs to feel safe and secure?

- Do household routines suit the child?

- Does the child treat the house like home?

"Significant others": are there significant other people who promote the child's sense of security? Or do they threaten it?

- Birth family members

- Child's friends

- Family friends

- Teachers

- Health professionals

- Social workers

- Therapists

- Any other significant figure in the child's life

The wider community: what does it offer to help the child feel secure?

- Is it generally an accepting community or is the child likely to be subject to disapproval or discrimination or the victim of bullying or crime?

- Do the carers participate in the life of the wider community?

- Are the carers and/or the child members of cultural and community organisations?

- Does the child take part in community activities?

When you have finished this exercise, you will have in front of you a visual map representing your assessment of the child's state of resilience and vulnerability. This is not a scientific exercise – it is just a tool to help you. With the information it brings out, you can plan how to work with the child and the network around him to reduce vulnerability and increase resilience.

SLIDE 29   Encouraging and enabling the network to promote resilience

- What impact do each of the key network members have in each domain?
  - Secure base
  - Education
  - Friendships
  - Talents and interests
  - Positive values
  - Social competencies
- What will enable them to promote resilience effectively for this child or young person?
- How can the child and carers engage these key people in the work of promoting resilience?

Explain the following to participants:

As part of this exercise, you have mapped the state of the child's resilience in each domain at the level of "carers" and "significant others".

Now think more specifically about the individual people whom you listed before the exercise. What impact does each of these people have in each domain? How could they promote resilience in the child or young person?

How can you, as the carer, and the child get these key people to understand the need to build the child's resilience and to work with you on this?

Exercise

Ask participants to rejoin the same groups they were in earlier, to discuss these questions. Each person in turn should share their thoughts with the people in their group; group members may be able to come up with other suggestions and ideas.

Exercise

In the same groups, ask participants to draw up a joint list of key people in the wider community who might have an impact on the resilience of the child or young person. Allow them around five minutes. When they have done this, ask them to briefly feed back their ideas. Write up their suggestions on the flipchart. Then show Slide 30, which lists some key people in this category.

SLIDE 30   The contribution of the wider community

- Who are key people in the wider community who have an impact on the resilience of this child or young person?
  - Children's services managers?
  - Fostering/residential care providers?
  - School/college management team or governors?
  - Health service providers or managers?
  - Local councillors?
  - Housing providers?
  - Employers?
  - Activity providers or cultural organisations?

Exercise

Ask the groups to consider: what ways could the child or young person and carers engage with people in the wider community? How could they get involved at this level in order to positively influence opportunities to build the child's resilience? For example, most local authorities and voluntary sector bodies have mechanisms for seeking the views of local people and service users. Carers might take part in local authority consultation exercises or user forums to make their views heard, or they could join the management committee of a youth group or other voluntary group that provides activities for young people. Young people could join a young people's panel or school council.

Allow them around five minutes. When they have done this, ask them to briefly feed back their ideas. Write up their suggestions on the flipchart. Then show Slide 31, which lists some more examples.

SLIDE 31   Engaging the community

- There may be interventions at the level of the whole community that will have a significant impact on the ability of this child or young person to build resilience and manage the transition to adult life
- Helping the child and carers or family members to undertake systemic interventions is a positive contribution to developing resilience
- Examples might include:
  - Approaching housing providers about special needs
  - Working with designated teachers to train school governors
  - Writing to senior managers in social care or health
  - Talking to local councillors about activities available locally

---

Some final points to make about resilience after trauma

Robbie Gilligan, who developed the concept of resilience in relation to traumatised children (2001), wrote:

A resilience-led perspective tends to be optimistic and pragmatic. It believes that change is often possible – even in unpromising conditions – and that it may start in simple ways.

Never forget that it takes courage, strength and resourcefulness to survive trauma in childhood. Whenever carers work with children and young people to promote resilience, this should be the starting point. Make sure the child knows that you recognise her resourcefulness and strength and celebrate her courage.

You cannot change her past, but together – and with the help of others – you can change her future.

61

Transitions and resilience

This article is adapted from Advanced Skills in Foster Care
Level 3 BTEC Qualification available online from Akamas
(Also available on the CD-ROM)

Introduction

Transitions occur throughout life. From the moment we are born our lives are marked by steps or stages that change us. Our development is not a straight line, but has distinct change points. Some of these transitions are a general part of human development for most people, such as:

● Walking

● Talking

● Puberty

● Becoming sexually active

● Becoming an adult

● Mid-life changes

● Old age

  Some transitions are socially determined, such as:

● Going to school

● Leaving school

● Going to college

● Entering employment

● Retirement

  Some transitions are culturally determined, such as:

● Religious conversion

● Initiation into a religious community

● Initiation into adult life

● Getting married

  Others are the result of individual circumstances, such as:

● Moving house

● Forming a new household

● Having a child

● Becoming unemployed

- Having a serious illness

- Having a serious accident

- Being involved in a disaster

All transitions change our lives. When they happen, even if they are longed for and welcomed, they make us feel unsettled. Life has changed, and there are always gains and losses to be integrated into our sense of self. We have to grieve for what has been lost, and adapt to what has been gained. Transitions are stressful.

The impact of transitions on traumatised children

Children who have not been able to benefit from the attachment process and develop stress regulation find all stressful experiences difficult to manage. And children who have lived through traumatic experiences will also have been injured in their ability to regulate stress. Even when they did develop stress regulation in their early years, traumatised children often lose that ability and find stressful situations overwhelming. So children who cannot regulate stress effectively find transitions very difficult.

Even ordinary transitions involve change and are therefore stressful. For children who cannot regulate stress, every transition may be traumatic.

About resilience

Different people have different abilities to manage transitions. And individual people have different abilities to manage different transitions. The key to understanding these differences is the concept of resilience.

Resilience is the ability to survive and thrive under difficult conditions. Resilient people can continue to develop to their own potential even when circumstances are against them. Resilience is not the same as coping. When we cope with difficulties we survive them, but sometimes at the cost of our own healthy development. When we are resilient we find ways of coping that allow us to continue to develop to our full potential.

Ecological perspective on the world of the child

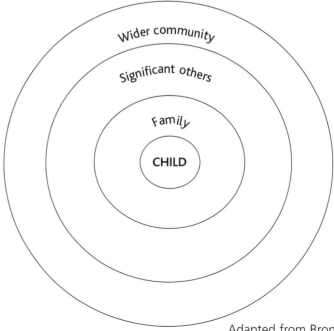

Adapted from Bronfenbrenner (1979)

Many factors contribute to resilience. Each person has around them a network of relationships. There are the close and intimate relationships of family and friends or kinship group, and then in widening circles there are more distant kinship and social groups, professionals with a duty of care such as doctors and teachers, the community in which we live, and finally the society of which that community is part. This is the ecology of human development (Bronfenbrenner, 1979).

Factors that help us to be resilient happen at all these levels. If these factors are absent we become vulnerable and may be harmed by transitions. If we have lots of personal strengths, and have supportive family and friends, and are well integrated into our community, and live in a reasonably stable society, we are more likely to survive difficult circumstances. If any of these levels are significantly diminished we are more vulnerable.

The nature of the transition event also makes a difference. Some events are more overwhelming than others.

In other words:

Some transition events are so terrible that most people would be harmed by them.

and

Some people are so vulnerable that most transition events will harm them.

It is important to remember that all of us all the time are both resilient and vulnerable. And our vulnerability and resilience never stay constant. They shift and change with circumstances and events. We are more vulnerable when we have a cold. We are more resilient when we have shared a good meal with friends. We do not seek to remove vulnerability, which would be impossible, but to reduce it and to increase resilience.

The strength and resourcefulness of traumatised children

'A resilience-led perspective tends to be optimistic and pragmatic. It believes that change is often possible – even in unpromising conditions – and that it may start in simple ways. From a resilience perspective, one thinks that the glass is half full rather than half empty.'

(Gilligan, 2001, p 7)

Many traumatised children are remarkably resilient. They seem to bounce back even from terrible events, and thrive in a secure and nurturing environment.

Others cope, but at the expense of their own healthy development. They survive, but their development has been injured by the harm they have suffered.

Some children may be resilient in some areas of their lives, but barely cope in others. They may, for example, be able to do well at school but be unable to manage the close relationships of a family. Or they may get on well at home, but be quite unable to manage the demands of school life.

It takes courage and strength and resourcefulness to survive trauma in childhood. Whenever carers work with children to promote resilience that resourcefulness and strength should be the starting point, and the courage of the child should be noted and celebrated.

The transition to adult life

Every successful transition the child makes helps to prepare them for the transition to adult life. Each time the child lives through a change event and emerges stronger and more resourceful, they are better able to face the challenge of the next change their life will bring.

Adults who understand the attachment process, the effects of unmet attachment needs and the importance of the life story are equipped to help the child develop resilience. This is the most effective preparation for adult life.

Factors that contribute to preparing children and young people for the transition to adult life

Research has identified a wide range of factors that contribute to building resilience. These occur at all ecological levels:

- Individual
- Family
- Significant others
- Wider community

These factors can be organised into six key areas or domains (Daniel and Wassell, 2002). Understanding the importance of each of these domains helps in assessing the resilience of a child and in planning how to enable the child to develop and build their resilience.

The six domains are:

- **Secure base**
  - The child has a sense of security
  - There is a stable attachment relationship with their carer or carers
  - Significant others are stable figures in the life of the child
  - The wider community is stable and supportive

- **Education**
  - The child is doing well in school
  - Carers support the child's education
  - Significant others support and contribute to the child's education
  - There is good local educational provision to meet the child's needs

- **Friendships**
  - The child understands friendship and can make and keep friends
  - Carers support the child's friendships
  - Significant others support the child's friendships
  - There are opportunities in the wider community for the child to make friends

- **Talents and interests**
  - The child has talents and interests
  - Carers support the child's talents and interests
  - Significant others support and contribute to the child's talents and interests
  - There are opportunities locally for the child to develop talents and interests

- **Positive values**
  - The child understands feelings and shows age-appropriate moral reasoning
  - Carers support and promote emotional literacy and moral reasoning
  - Significant others support the development of positive values
  - The wider community promotes positive values

- **Social competencies**
  - The child shows appropriate autonomy and self-belief
  - Carers promote the social competence of the child
  - Significant others support the development of social competence
  - The wider community provides opportunities for the child to practise social competence

There are clear links between these domains and the seven dimensions of child development identified for the Looking After Children System. The difference is that the LAC System was based on the criteria parents use for assessing the outcome of their parenting, whilst the domains of resilience are based on the factors that contribute to children being able to survive and thrive in difficult circumstances.

It will be clear from your study of attachment that having a secure base is the foundation upon which all the other domains depend. If the child or young person does not have a secure base they will be more vulnerable.

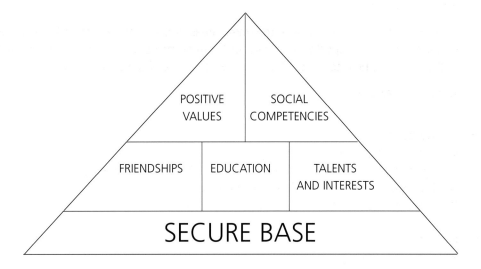

Article

Mapping resilience

This article is adapted from Advanced Skills in Foster Care
Level 3 BTEC Qualification available online from Akamas
(Also available on the CD-ROM)

Think about a child or young person you know who is adopted or is in foster care or residential care.

As you progress through the rest of this session you will be forming an assessment of the child's resilience and vulnerability. This is not a formal assessment, but is a working tool for you to use to plan how you can enable the child to develop resilience.

Using the resilience chart you will be able to mark the resilience of the child in each domain and at each ecological level, using a simple green/amber/red code. You will be asked to decide whether in your opinion the child is resilient (green), coping (amber) or vulnerable (red) in that domain and at that level. For example, in the domain of secure base, use all that you have learned about attachment to help you assess the resilience of the child you have in mind.

As you think about the points that follow, decide whether the child is in your opinion resilient, coping or vulnerable in relation to having each domain at each ecological level.

When you have formed your opinion about this you can fill in the secure base part of the chart. Using the traffic light colour code, where

- Green = resilient

- Amber = coping

- Red = vulnerable

Fill in each cell of the chart with the appropriate colour. For example, if you think the child or young person is at present vulnerable in their own sense of a secure base, you would colour the "child" segment red.

They may have a friend who has moved away, making them more vulnerable at the level of "significant others". But they may also have an adult older sister who is very supportive, a teacher they like and trust, a mentor who is helpful and a therapist who is enabling the child to make progress with grieving. So on balance you would colour the "significant others" segment green.

Use all that you have learned about attachment to help you assess the resilience of the child you have in mind in the domain of secure base. As you think about the points that follow, decide whether the child is in your opinion resilient, coping or vulnerable in relation to having a secure base and at each ecological level.

If you are the carers for this child, take the opportunity to reflect on the care you provide as though you were an outsider. If you are thinking about a child known to you but cared for by others, use this opportunity to think about the experience of the carers as well as the experience of the child.

Do this exercise with the child or young person you have in mind if at all possible. It will still be your opinion that is being reflected, but you will be able to discuss it with them and gain an understanding of their own view of their state of being. Or see if they would like to fill it in for themselves and then compare the two results. Resilience is a transformative idea. It allows the child or young person to see themselves, and to be seen, as:

- Normal
  - Everyone is vulnerable.

- Hopeful
  - Vulnerability and resilience are always changing. We can always become more resilient.

- Strong
  - To have survived at all shows that they can cope. Coping can always be transformed into resilience.

When you have finished the whole exercise you will have in front of you a visual map representing your assessment of the child's state of resilience and vulnerability. Remember, this is not a scientific exercise. It is just a tool for you to think effectively about the resilience and vulnerability of the child so that you can better help them to become more resilient. The information you can draw from this should help you to plan how to work with the child and the network around the child to reduce vulnerability and increase resilience.

Secure base

Examples of some points you might want to consider:

- What is the evidence that the child feels secure or insecure?
  - How does the child react to stress?
  - Do they seek help if they experience stress? To whom do they turn?
  - Do they try to be in control of other people?
  - Do they seem confident that they will have the attention of adults when needed?

- What is the evidence that the people caring for the child provide a secure base?
  - Are the carers able to show commitment to the child?
  - Does the environment meet the needs of the child to feel safe and secure?
  - Do household routines suit the child?
  - Does the child treat the environment as home?

- Are there significant other people who affect the sense of security of the child?
  - Birth family members?
  - Friends of the child?
  - Friends of the family?
  - Teachers?
  - Health professionals?
  - Social workers?
  - Therapists?
  - Is there a current list of all the significant people in the life of the child?

- What opportunities are there in the wider community to help the child feel secure?
  - Is it generally an accepting community?
  - Do the carers participate in the life of the wider community?
  - Is membership of cultural and community organisations valued by the carers?
  - Does the child take part in community activities?
  - Is the child included in a faith community?

And so on. You may have other ideas. It might be useful to discuss your ideas and discoveries with other students.

Education

There is evidence from research that educational attainment is a powerful resilience factor (Jackson, 2001).

Examples of some points you might want to consider:

- What is the evidence about the educational attainment of the child?
  - Does the child seem interested in their environment?
  - Do they seem happy with their preschool/school/college?
  - Are they included in mainstream education/preschool?
  - Do they seem to enjoy learning?
  - Do they have educational hopes and ambitions?

- What is the evidence that the people caring for the child are helping the child's cognitive development?
  - Do carers attend preschool/school/college functions?
  - Do they take an interest in the child's learning?
  - Do they actively help and encourage the child to learn?
  - Do the carers model learning as an enjoyable activity?
  - Does the environment support learning with books, computer, and so on?

- Are there significant other people who affect the educational attainments of the child?
  - Do members of the child's birth family support the child's education?
  - Does the child have friends who enjoy education and actively learn?
  - Does the child have a role model for learning and educational attainment?
  - Are there any teachers the child particularly likes?
  - Does the child have a mentor?

- What opportunities are there in the wider community to help the child's cognitive development?
  - Does the community offer educational activities out of school?
  - Does the child use a library service?
  - Does the child belong to any community groups that promote learning?
  - Are the child's teachers part of the local community?

And so on.

Friendships

Examples of some points you might want to consider:

- What is the evidence that this child understands friendship and can make and keep friends?
  - Do they have lasting friendships?
  - Do they think of themselves as being a good friend?
  - Do they value friendships?
  - Do they in conversation show an age-appropriate understanding of friendships?
  - Are their friends significantly older or younger than they are?
  - Do their carers like their friends?

- What is the evidence that the people caring for the child are helping the child to develop positive friendships?
  - Do the carers like the child's friends?
  - Do friends visit the child at home?
  - Is the child encouraged to spend time with friends?
  - Are there conversations at home about friends and friendship?
  - Do the carers have friends?

- Are there significant other people who affect the ability of the child to make and keep friends?
  - Do members of the birth family encourage the child to value friendships?
  - Does the child come from a friendly family?
  - Is the child being victimised, bullied or marginalised?
  - Does the child seem to fit in with their peers? Do they present themselves appropriately?

- What opportunities are there in the wider community to help the child develop friendships?
  - Is the child a member of friendly organisations?
  - Are there opportunities in the community for the child to meet and to make friends, such as clubs, sports facilities and teams, out of school activities, faith based groups, and so on?

Talents and interests

Self-esteem is fundamental to resilience. Talents and interests build self-esteem.

Case study

Donna, aged nine, is placed in a foster family after many years of undetected abuse and neglect. This included locking her in the house so that she could not go to school but would take care of her younger brothers and sisters. In the foster home she shows many difficult behaviours. But she loves going to school and begins to do well there.

The school has a brass band which Donna joins. She discovers a talent for playing brass instruments. Soon she is invited to join a brass consort of some reputation. Her carers find a special bursary fund locally for gifted children, and use the money to buy her a trumpet.

The discovery of Donna's talent brings her both friends and increased self-esteem. Her resilience is increased.

Examples of some points you might want to consider:

- What is the evidence that this child has any talents or special interests?
  - What are they good at?
  - What are they interested in?
  - What do they do that makes them feel good about themselves?
  - Is there anything they dream of doing?

- What is the evidence that the people caring for the child are helping the child to develop their talents, are supporting their interests and encouraging them to experiment with new interests?
  - Do the carers know what the child can do, would like to do, and enjoys doing?
  - Do they offer practical support to help the child pursue their interests and develop their talents?
  - Does the home environment stimulate ideas for new interests and hobbies?
  - Do the carers pursue interests and talents of their own?

- Are there significant other people who affect the ability of the child to explore and express their talents and interests?
  - Do members of the child's birth family support and encourage the child's talents and interests?
  - Does the child have friends who have special talents or pursue interests?
  - Does the child have a role model for being talented or enjoying pursuing interests?
  - Is there anyone who actively discourages the child from believing in themselves or following their interests?

- What opportunities are there in the wider community to help the child explore and express their talents and interests?
  - Is it a community that has open access for children to such activities as sports, music making, drama, art, crafts, and so on?
  - Is it a community in which such activities are valued?
  - Does the child feel included in the opportunities the community offers?
  - Is there funding available for the child to pursue talents, hobbies and interests?

Positive values

In resilience work, having positive values is shown by an age-appropriate capacity to help others, comfort others, share with others, understand other perspectives and apply moral reasoning. Children with such values are more resilient.

Moral reasoning normally changes as the child develops. Lawrence Kohlberg developed a theory of moral stages which is explored and set in a broader developmental context by Ken Wilber (2001, chapter 4):

- **Preconventional morality**
  - Young children begin to grasp the concept of consequences. They do not understand rules, but believe that what is right is what is permitted by their carers and what is wrong is what is prohibited by their carers.
    - Focus on punishment
  - If their needs are being met and they are developing healthily, they begin to apply a judgment about their own interests. Rules are beginning to be recognised and they are followed when it is to the immediate benefit of the child.
    - Focus on reward

- **Conventional morality**
  - In middle childhood many children develop a moral sense based on recognising that other people have expectations of them which it is right to live up to. Qualities that support group solidarity, such as loyalty, are valued.
    - Focus on relationships
  - They may then develop to the next stage, of recognising that social rules and promises are important and should be kept.
    - Focus on social order

- **Postconventional morality**
  - Some young people go on to develop moral reasoning based on an understanding that rules are relative to a group and human rights take precedence.
    - Focus on rights
  - A few develop moral reasoning based on a coherent value system relying on universal ethical principles
    - Focus on truth and justice

When children develop they do not stop being able to function at an earlier level – they gain an ability to function at a later level of development. If they, or we, or anyone suffers trauma or unbearable adversity, we may regress to an earlier stage. We may have strong principles, but under certain pressures we can become egocentric or rigid and rule-dominated.

When assessing the moral reasoning of older children, it is useful to know not only what level of reasoning they currently produce but also to get an idea of whether they have ever been capable of more highly developed reasoning. Are we trying to help them develop new abilities or to recover existing ones temporarily lost?

Examples of some points you might want to consider:

- What is the evidence that this child can engage in age-appropriate:
  - Moral reasoning?
  - Understanding other perspectives?
  - Caring for others?
  - Sharing with others?

- What is the evidence that the people caring for the child are helping the child to develop moral values?
  - Do the carers provide role models for developed moral thought?
  - Are there conversations about positive values?
  - Is caring for others encouraged?
  - Is sharing encouraged?
  - Is the child valued for their efforts to develop values?

- Are there significant other people who affect the ability of the child to develop moral values?
  - Do members of the child's birth family encourage the child to develop positive values?
  - Does the child have friends who have positive values?
  - Does the child have any role model for developing positive values?
  - Is there anyone who actively discourages the child from developing positive values?

- What opportunities are there in the wider community to help the child develop positive values?
  - Are there groups or organisations encouraging the development of positive values in the community?
  - Does the child have a mentor or personal adviser?
  - Is the family part of a faith group?
  - Is the child part of a faith group?
  - Are there opportunities in the community for the child to help others?

Social competencies

Social competence is a very broad area of human experience and behaviour. The elements of it that seem most relevant for developing resilience are:

- Autonomy: being able and willing to take responsibility for the self
- Self-control: being able to control and regulate our own behaviour
- Self-efficacy: believing that we can be effective in the world
- Attention: being able to concentrate

Examples of some points you might want to consider:

- How would you describe this child in relation to:
  - Autonomy?
  - Self-control?
  - Self-efficacy?
  - Attention?

- What is the evidence that the people caring for the child are helping the child to develop social competencies?
  - Do carers accept and encourage autonomy in the child?
  - Do carers actively help the child to develop self-control?
  - Do carers show self-control in their own behaviour?
  - Is the child helped to notice when they have acted effectively?
  - Does the environment promote attentiveness and concentration?

- Are there significant other people who affect the ability of the child to develop social competencies?
  - Do members of the child's birth family help the child to develop social competencies?
  - Does the child have friends who help the child develop social competencies?
  - Does the child have a role model for social competence?
  - Are there any particular teachers, mentors, play leaders who help the child or share activities with the child that promote social competencies?

- What opportunities are there in the wider community to help the child develop their social competencies?
  - Does the child belong to community groups?
  - Is there a wide range of groups and activities available for the child to join?
  - Is there a range of faith groups within the community that the child would be allowed to join?

3 Healing environments

What is a healing environment?

This is the first session of the third part of the course, so welcome the participants and put them at their ease.

Explain what they can expect from the course – that there will be some direct input from you, in terms of your slide presentation, but that they also have a lot to contribute from their own knowledge and experience. Explain that they will not simply be sitting and listening to you – they will be actively involved in discussion and group exercises, coming up with their own thoughts, ideas and suggestions.

Introductions

If any participants are new to the group and did not attend earlier sessions, ask participants to introduce themselves to the rest of the group.

Ground rules

You may want to reiterate the ground rules that were set out at the start of Session A in Part 1 of this course – *Trauma*.

Provide the handout

Give participants a handout of the slide presentation so that they do not need to write everything down – they can make additional notes on their handout if this is helpful.

SLIDE 1 **Learning outcomes**

- **To understand the links between the physical environment and healing**
- **To recognise the characteristics of a healing environment**
- **To analyse the needs of a traumatised child**
- **To think of ways to promote healing environments for a traumatised child**

This slide presents the learning outcomes for Sessions A and B of *Healing Environments*.

SLIDE 2 **What is a healing environment?**

In this session, we will be thinking about:

- The impact of sensory information on our sense of wellbeing.

- What traumatised children need from their physical environment.

SLIDES 3, 4 and 5

- Traumatic stress begins in the environment
- An event in the external world reaches the brain as sensory information
- The response to this information overwhelms the ability to self-regulate a range of functions such as:
  - Stress
  - Mood
  - Impulse
  - Language
- Sensory information has a powerful impact

- Traumatic stress changes blood supply to the brain, causing lasting injury
- Children disordered after traumatic stress find it difficult or impossible to regulate stress
- They may never have developed stress regulation patterns in the brain because their need for soothing in infancy was not met
  - Developmental trauma
- They may have lived through terrifying experiences such as abuse or exploitation
  - Emotional trauma

- Children with stress disorders may be:

  Hyperaroused

  Aware of discomfort and distress

  Behaving in a distressed manner

  Hyperactive/unable to concentrate/poor sleep

  Aggressive/destructive/self-harming

  Dissociated

  Cut off from sensory experience

  Not behaving in a distressed manner

  Controlling/compliant/withdrawn

  Unable to recognise sensory clues (hot/cold, hunger . . .)

If participants have attended the previous course on *Trauma*, they will be familiar with these concepts. If they have not, you will need to spend some time explaining them.

SLIDE 6   What is stress regulation?

- Think of one activity that helps you to regulate stress
  - What exactly happens in your body as the stress becomes regulated?
  - What do you feel?
  - How do you know when the stress level has reduced?
- Discuss your ideas with others around you
- What are the key points arising from your discussion?

Explain that emotional trauma disrupts many areas of human function – such as empathy, rational thinking, language, memory, attention, concentration, ability to regulate mood and impulse, and so on. But the most basic and crucial of all these changes is the loss of the ability to regulate stress. People who have developed post-traumatic stress disorders need, before all else, to recover this ability.

The following exercise encourages participants to think about the physical and emotional correlates of stress and stress reduction.

Exercise

If participants are sitting in groups at tables, ask each group to discuss the questions on Slide 6 for a few minutes. (*What exactly happens in your body as the stress becomes regulated? What do you feel? How do you know when the stress level has reduced?*)

If they are not at tables, ask them to work in threes or fours with the people sitting close to them.

Afterwards, ask each group to feed back one key point to the group as a whole. Write the key points on the flipchart. Continue to ask each group in turn to add another key point until they have all shared all their ideas.

SLIDE 7   Indicators of stress regulation

- **Breathing slows down and moves deeper**
- **Pulse rate slows down**
- **Skin feels softer, and may feel warmer or cooler**
- **Muscle tone changes and becomes less tense**
    Limbs may feel heavier or lighter
    Face muscles soften
- **Things look different**
- **Things sound different**
- **Feelings change**

These points may well have emerged during the previous exercise.

- Breathing slows down and, rather than the "shallow breathing" of stress, it comes from deeper into the chest/abdominal cavity

- Things look different – when no longer preoccupied or distracted by stress, it may be easier to see your environment in general, or to focus on specific aspects of your environment. What you see may seem to have a different quality.

- Things sound different – you may hear sounds you had not noticed when stressed, or the sounds may seem to have a different quality or timbre.

- Feelings change – you may feel peaceful, tranquil, with a sense of tension ebbing away. You may be alert and more aware of your surroundings, or as you relax you may be drowsy and aware of inner release. Some people experience an "oceanic" sense of connectedness.

Sensory experience that arouses a reaction in the sympathetic nervous system produces stimulation; sensory experience that reduces arousal in the sympathetic nervous system and arouses a reaction in the parasympathetic system produces soothing.

In times of stress, anger or fear, the sympathetic nervous system produces large doses of stress hormones such as adrenaline and cortisol. In contrast, when we are relaxed and happy, the parasympathetic system produces a range of pleasure hormones called endorphins.

People suffering from post-traumatic stress have lost the ability to regulate stress or to produce these pleasure hormones.

SLIDE 8   Five senses and more

- Each of our senses is involved in the processes of stimulation and relaxation
  - Vision
  - Hearing
  - Smell
  - Taste
  - Touch
- Additional sensory information also contributes:
  - Proxemics (distance between self and others)
  - Temperature
  - And so on

Our awareness of where we are and what is going on around us is drawn from sensory information. Human beings react to their environment. This sensory information helps to determine how stimulated or relaxed we feel at any given time.

Think about the methods used by those who wish to interrogate or torture others or destroy their spirit. They use harsh environments, bare walls, bright lights, sometimes loud noise or the sound of other people screaming. Sometimes they use sensory deprivation – silence, darkness, isolation.

Equally, an environment can be designed to maximise healing and recovery.

Hospitals and other care settings are becoming more aware of the factors in the physical environment that can promote health and are exploring things like the effect of having art and poetry on the walls. Richard Mazuch is an architectural design consultant who specialises in "sense-sensitive design" for hospitals and mental health facilities. Participants who are interested in this issue can find out more on the internet.

Ask participants to reflect on how much nicer it would feel to be in a hospital ward if the temperature is just right, your bed is comfortable and not too close to the next patient, there are cheerful curtains at the window and you can listen to music and enjoy a view of the sky and trees outside.

SLIDES 9 to 14

Exercise

The following exercise will encourage participants to think of times when different types of sensory information caused them to feel either stressed or relaxed.

Ask participants to work in small groups of, say, three or four. Say that you would like each participant to try to think of an example from his or her own experience. Some people may find it difficult to think of an example for each of the senses. If they can't come up with anything, they can simply join in the discussion of the experiences of other members of their group.

At the end of the whole exercise – when they have discussed the five senses plus proximity – ask them to share their examples with the whole group. Ask each group in turn to call out their ideas. Ask each group in turn to feed back their thoughts for each exercise in turn, rather than covering all six in one go. Make it clear that if there are some experiences participants shared with their small group but would not feel comfortable feeding back to the whole group, this is fine.

The range of ideas that participants think of will immediately make it clear how personal these matters are. Some people find camomile tea relaxing, others hate it. For some people there is nothing more relaxing than to sit and stroke a cat, while others can't stand cats.

Explain that the interaction between the environment and the individual is unique. But it is always an interaction. Each person is constantly physically changed by the impact their environment has on them. And what changes us physically can heal us when we need healing.

Below you will find some ideas which you can present to get the ball rolling at the start or to add when participants are feeding back.

SLIDE 9   Stress and relaxation: Vision

- **Think of an occasion when an experience involving the sense of sight caused a change in your body that was:**
  Stressful
  Relaxing
  - **If you have difficulty doing this exercise ask someone nearby to do it with you and interview them about their experiences**
- **Discuss with others both the memories and the effect in the present of remembering these experiences**
- **What are the key points arising?**

Relaxing:

- Sunrise or sunset

- A work of art

- The face of someone we love

- A beautiful view

Stressful:

- Harrowing images in the newspaper or on television

- The face of someone who frightens us or whom we dislike

- Some artificial lighting

SLIDE 10   Stress and relaxation: Hearing

- Think of an occasion when an experience involving the sense of hearing caused a change in your body that was:
  Stressful
  Relaxing
  - If you have difficulty doing this exercise ask someone nearby to do it with you and interview them about their experiences
- Discuss with others both the memories and the effect in the present of remembering these experiences
- What are the key points arising?

Relaxing:

- Tranquil music
- The sound of the voice of someone we love
- The sound of the sea
- The sound of birdsong

Stressful:

- Loud discordant music
- The sound of the voice of someone who frightens you or whom you dislike
- The sound of a siren or alarm

SLIDE 11   Stress and relaxation: Smell

- Think of an occasion when an experience involving the sense of smell caused a change in your body that was:
  Stressful
  Relaxing
  - If you have difficulty doing this exercise ask someone nearby to do it with you and interview them about their experiences
- Discuss with others both the memories and the effect in the present of remembering these experiences
- What are the key points arising?

Relaxing:

- The scent of the sea
- The scent of grass
- The scent of certain flowers
- The scent of home cooking

Stressful:

- The smell of disinfectant in hospital
- The smell of vomit
- The smell of traffic fumes

SLIDE 12   Stress and relaxation: Taste

- Think of an occasion when an experience involving the sense of taste caused a change in your body that was:
  Stressful
  Relaxing
    - If you have difficulty doing this exercise ask someone nearby to do it with you and interview them about their experiences
- Discuss with others both the memories and the effect in the present of remembering these experiences
- What are the key points arising?

Relaxing:

- Chocolate
- Camomile tea
- Vanilla
- Familiar home-cooked food

Stressful:

- Unfamiliar food
- Bitter coffee
- Any taste associated with illness

SLIDE 13   Stress and relaxation: Touch

- Think of an occasion when an experience involving the sense of touch caused a change in your body that was:
  Stressful
  Relaxing
    - If you have difficulty doing this exercise ask someone nearby to do it with you and interview them about their experiences
- Discuss with others both the memories and the effect in the present of remembering these experiences
- What are the key points arising?

Relaxing:

- Stroking or being stroked by someone you love
- Stroking an animal
- Stroking a beautiful surface such as satin or wood

- Being in water

- Being at just the right temperature

Stressful:

- Being touched by someone who frightens you or whom you dislike

- Touching something unfamiliar and unexpected

- Touching animals you find repellent such as snakes or spiders

- Being at an uncomfortable temperature

SLIDE 14   Stress and relaxation: Proxemics

- **Think of an occasion when an experience involving the sense of distance from others caused a change in your body that was:**
  Stressful
  Relaxing
  - **If you have difficulty doing this exercise ask someone nearby to do it with you and interview them about their experiences**
- **Discuss with others both the memories and the effect in the present of remembering these experiences**
- **What are the key points arising?**

Relaxing:

- Being able to choose how close you are to other people

- Being in a public space where you feel comfortable with the distance between people

- Being able to be close to people you love when in a strange environment

Stressful:

- Having to be too close to other people

- Having to be far apart from people you know or love when you are in a strange place

SLIDE 15   Stress regulation and the environment

- **The interaction between the environment and the individual is unique**
- **Each person is constantly changed by the impact their environment has on them**
- **Such changes affect our physical, psychological, emotional and social functioning**
- **Most people can maintain their own equilibrium even in difficult environments**
- **Traumatised people often find it difficult to regulate stress and maintain equilibrium**
  - **The physical environment has a powerful effect on them**

Use the results of the previous exercise to illustrate the points on this slide. Participants will have come up with very individual ideas about experiences that are stressful or relaxing.

Whether we are aware of it or not, we are constantly affected by the physical environment. It can affect the way we feel physically, our mood, our emotions and the way we interact with other people. Some environments can feel like an assault on the senses – being in a nightclub with strobe lights and a thumping techno soundtrack or Christmas shopping at 5 pm on Christmas Eve, for example.

Most of us can somehow cope even in environments that make us feel uncomfortable – for instance, if they are too noisy, too crowded or too hot. But people who have been traumatised can find it difficult to manage the stress of being in a difficult environment and can find it overwhelming. Because they do not have ways of regulating their own stress effectively, they are at the mercy of the physical environment.

In general, traumatised children are reactive through the sympathetic nervous system, even to stimuli that in others would elicit parasympathetic responses. They are hypersensitive – this is why traumatised children are often overwhelmed by sensory experience that has no effect on other children. It is this hypersensitivity that we can try to soothe by making changes in their environment.

When children are dissociated, however, they are disconnected from their own sensory experience. We need to help them regain connection. Again, we can do this by making changes in their environment – this time by providing a more stimulating environment.

In the next exercise we will look at the types of sensory information that might have an effect on a child.

SLIDE 16   ## Making sense of the environment: a guided tour of your experience

- **Call to mind one room in which you have worked with a traumatised child**
  - **Think of each of the five senses in relation to this room**
    What does it look like?
    What sounds do you associate with this space?
    Are there any scents you associate with the room?
    Is this a space associated with particular food or drink?
    What textures, surfaces, temperature, fabrics, distance from others and so on do you associate with this space?
  - **What is the overall sensory impact of this room on you?**
- **Discuss with others and note any key points**

Exercise

Ask participants to think about the questions on Slide 16 and to discuss this with the others in their small group. Do not ask for feedback.

Now ask them to suggest as many factors as possible that affect a child's experiences in an environment. Think about each of the senses, plus proximity, in turn.

Ask participants to call out their ideas while you write them up on the flip chart. For each factor, establish whether it would be soothing or stimulating.

Some of the factors that you and the participants might suggest are listed below:

VISION

- **Light**

  - Natural light or artificial light

  - Full spectrum (like daylight) or part spectrum (like most artificial light)

  NB Seasonal Affective Disorder (SAD) is a psychiatric condition affected by changes in daylight and treated through the use of full spectrum light

  - Coloured light: bulbs, filters and gels

NB Coloured light has been used effectively with some children with autistic spectrum disorder

- Polarised light: sunglasses, windscreens

- Reflected light and direct light

NB Our ordinary vision comes from reflected light, but television and VDUs involve looking directly at light sources

- Electric light, gaslight, candlelight, firelight

- **Colour**

  - Walls, ceilings, floors, furnishings, clothes

  - Primary colours, pastel colours, black, white

  - Intensity of colour

  - Combinations of colour

  - Plain or patterned

- **Surfaces**

  - Matt, glossy, absorbing or reflecting light

  - Rough or smooth

  - Natural or synthetic

- **Shape**

  - Straight lines, circles, curves

  - Angular shapes and organic shapes

  - Two dimensions and three dimensions

- **Vista**

  - Short focus or long focus

    - Generally the eye relaxes to longer focus, and when the eye relaxes the body relaxes

    - Movement between short and long focus may be most relaxing

    - Windows, mirrors, three-dimensional objects and pictures with vista can all allow the eye to relax

- **Movement within the field of vision**

  - Stillness

  - Gentle movement

  - Hectic movement

- **Images**
  - Natural images
    - Trees, rural scenes, sea, lakes, people, animals, night-time, daytime
  - Constructed images
    - Buildings, mechanical objects, urban scenes
  - Paintings, photographs, murals
    - Art therapy may help traumatised children to connect to their visual sensory experience as well as to express experience through different media

- **Surroundings**
  - Interior space
    - Rooms, corridors
    - Size, shapes, proportions
  - Exterior space
    - Shared entrances, courtyards, gardens, patios
    - Size, shapes, proportions
  - Surrounding landscape
    - Urban, suburban, rural
    - Streets, hills, mountains, moors, fields, lakes, sea

HEARING

- **Ambient sound, the underlying sounds in an environment**
  - Traumatised children may, for example, be sensitive to noise generated by:
    - Refrigerators or freezers
    - Road traffic
    - Trains
    - Aeroplanes
    - Plumbing
    - Other people talking, laughing or singing
    - Background noise from radios and televisions
    - Drills or lawnmowers

- **Sound quality**
  - Gentle or harsh
  - Loud or soft
  - High-pitched or low-pitched
  - Pure or complex

- **Music**
  - Type of music
  - Volume: loud or soft
  - Rhythm: rapid or slow
  - Live or recorded

    NB Music therapy has been used with children with attachment disorders

- **Voice**
  - Male or female
  - High-pitched or low-pitched
  - Timbre: the message of the voice quality
  - Familiar language patterns
  - Familiar accents

- **Rhythm**
  - The impact of rhythmic sounds in the environment, such as clocks ticking
  - The use of rhythm such as hand-clapping when telling stories or reciting poetry
  - Rhythmic movement to sound, dance

- **Silence**
  - The impact of the absence of sound on the child

SMELL AND TASTE

Remember that traumatised children often have reduced function in the thinking brain, the neocortex, and increased function in the reactive and impulsive limbic brain. In that condition they may be hypersensitive to smell and taste. Their senses may be working like the senses of a baby.

- **Basic scents or odours associated with particular settings**
  - At home:
    - Entrances, the first smell on entering
    - Living space in the home
    - Bedroom
    - Bathroom
    - Cooking and eating areas
  - At school:
    - Entrances, the first smell on entering
    - Classrooms
    - Changing areas
    - Sports areas
    - Cooking and eating areas
  - At the swimming baths
  - And so on

- **Specific aromas**
  - Natural scents in particular places: plants, flowers, grass, hay
  - Artificial scents: air fresheners, cleaning agents
  - Smells of familiar food
  - Smells of soothing drinks such as hot chocolate

- **Body odour, which is unique to each individual and an important part of the attachment process**
  - As children form a positive attachment to their carers the body odour of the carer will become soothing for the child
  - Objects used by the carer may be soothing
    - Clothing such as T-shirts, scarves, gloves
    - Fabric such as pillow cases

  NB Scent used by a carer may be sprayed on familiar objects such as a school bag or scarf

- **Animals**
  - If the child forms a relationship with an animal, they may be soothed by carrying something that smells of the animal, such as a small piece of blanket

- Taste

    - What flavours could be associated with the space?

    - Special bedtime drinks

    - Popcorn when watching television

    - Ice cream in the garden

TOUCH AND PROXIMITY

Like smell and taste, the sensory experiences of touch and proximity are very primitive, and may be particularly sensitive in traumatised children.

- **Texture of walls, floors, objects**

    We are in touch with our physical environment more than we usually realise. People can orientate themselves in space by the texture of familiar floors, for example:

    - Natural or synthetic material

    - Rough or smooth

    - Soft or hard

    - Felt with the hands, feet, or whole body

- **Surfaces of furniture, floors, objects**

    Every physical thing has a surface, and every surface may be touched. The nature of the surface will determine whether for any person the touch is stimulant or soothing

    - Natural or synthetic material

    - Rounded or sharp-edged

    - Straight lines or organic forms

    - Hard or soft

- **Temperature**

    - Cold, warm or hot

    - Comfortable or uncomfortable

- **Fabrics**

    Babies love to stroke fabrics, and so do many traumatised children

    - Natural or synthetic material

    - Rough or smooth

    - Soft or stiff and unyielding

    - Plain or with holes and patterns

    - Felt with hands, feet, or whole body

- **Water**

  Water can be very frightening for some traumatised children, especially if they were abused in bathrooms, but it can also be very soothing

  - Cold, warm or hot

  - Still (like a bath) or moving (like a shower)

  - Deep or shallow

  - Rain and snow, and other outdoor water

- **Moving air**

  Traumatised children often respond to moving air

  - Fans

  - Hairdryers

  - Wind in the open air

- **Skin, hair and fur**

  Contact with other humans or animals can be stimulating or soothing

  - Touching other people

  - Doing hair for other people

  - Stroking animals

- **Pillows, cushions and duvets**

  Children and young people will often hug a pillow or cushion, or snuggle into a duvet

  - Size and shape

  - Firm or yielding

  - Nature of covering fabric

- **Proximity**

  Traumatised children often find closeness threatening, and those who are beginning to form attachments may find distance frightening. Eye contact, in situations where people are brought face to face, is stimulating and many traumatised children cannot cope with it at all. Traumatised children often feel more comfortable when close to but not face-to-face with others. On the other hand they may just feel disorientated.

  - Areas of the environment where people are brought close together by the architecture or the arrangement of furniture

  - Areas of the environment where people are kept far apart by the architecture or the arrangement of furniture

> - Areas where people are brought face-to-face
>
> - Areas where people are side by side, or facing in different directions
>
> Remember that dissociated children who are disconnected from their own responses may still be aroused by the sensory experience but unable to recognise the arousal. So hyperaroused children are unable to regulate the arousal, and dissociated children are unable either to recognise or to regulate the arousal.

SLIDE 17   Making sense of the environment: the child's experience

- **Think of a traumatised child or young person known to you**
- **Return to the previous exercise and think again about the room you have in mind**
- **Repeat the sensory tour of the environment as though you were the child or young person**
  - **What do you think is the overall sensory impact of this room on the traumatised child or young person?**
- **Discuss with others and note key points and issues**

Exercise

Now show participants Slide 17 and ask them to repeat the "guided tour" of the room they had in mind earlier. However, this time you want them to imagine they are exploring it through the senses of a traumatised child or young person they know. They should bear in mind all the factors that you have just mentioned (above) and consider the overall sensory impact of the room on the child or young person.

Each participant can do this on an individual basis and then they can discuss their thoughts with the rest of their small group.

Ask each small group to share one key point or interesting example with the whole group.

SLIDE 18   What do children need in order to recover from trauma?

- **Stabilisation**
  - **Feeling safe, gaining insight into own functioning, learning or relearning words for feelings**
- **Integration**
  - **Developing self-regulation, processing emotions and restructuring distorted thinking**
- **Adaptation**
  - **Establishing social connectedness and building self-esteem and joy in living**
- **Creating a healing environment is the lowest level intervention to promote and sustain this process**

Remind participants about the material on Slides 4 and 5 on traumatised children, stress regulation, hyperarousal and dissociation.

Recovering from trauma involves three stages: stabilisation, integration and adaptation (see earlier sessions on trauma for further explanation if necessary), and there are many ways for carers to help the child through these processes.

The physical environments the child spends time in on a day-to-day basis can either help or hinder. One of the simplest and most basic ways a carer can help is to provide the child with a physical environment which has the right conditions to promote recovery. Ideally, you will be able to plan and create this with input from the child.

SLIDE 19   Making spaces that work for traumatised children

- **Traumatised children are hypersensitive to their environment**
- **They become hyperaroused in response to minor changes**
- **Hyperaroused children need an environment that SOOTHES**
  - **Dissociation is an automatic protective response**
  - **Some traumatised children dissociate and disconnect from their sensory experience**
  - **They need to reconnect before they can benefit from soothing**
- **Dissociated children need an environment that STIMULATES**

Traumatised children are often hypersensitive to their environment and even minor things which would not bother any other child can trigger a reaction or problem behaviour. They react to stimulus as babies do, without being able to process the experience through their "thinking" brain.

If a traumatised child is hyperaroused, she will need an environment that *soothes* the arousal.

On the other hand, if a child is dissociated, she needs an environment that *stimulates* instead. Remind participants that dissociated children are not aware of their feelings – even in terms of basic things like whether they are too hot or too cold. They are "cut off" from the world. They need to reconnect with their sensory experience and they need an environment which will promote this.

Tell participants that in the next session they will learn how to plan the features of an environment so that it meets the child's needs.

3 Healing environments

Planning the healing environment

SLIDE 20   **Planning the healing environment**

In the mid-twentieth century there was a movement to bring together psychology, psychiatry and the environment as a way of treating children who were psychologically disturbed.

In the United States, Bruno Bettelheim established something called Milieu Therapy (1974) (*milieu* is another word for environment). In England, therapeutic communities were set up for children, incorporating something called Planned Environment Therapy. Children were in the therapeutic setting 24 hours a day, seven days a week. The idea was that if children have become unable to manage any ordinary environment without becoming completely overwhelmed, a setting like this might bring them the calm and stability they need.

But in the 1980s there was a move towards evidence-based practice and there was not enough scientific evidence showing the benefits of the milieu therapy approach. At the same time there was a move away from residential child care towards family-based care. So Planned Environment Therapy lost its appeal and its influence.

Nowadays we are clearer about the potential for living in an institution to have harmful effects on children and there is a clear preference for placement in foster care if at all possible, provided the child can be kept safe in a family setting. The result of this is that most traumatised children, like the rest of us, live in an ordinary home in an ordinary community and spend time in a number of different places during the course of the day or week – home, school, friends' houses, youth club.

When we are thinking about making the child's environment more therapeutic and making changes that will help him recover, we need to think about the effect of spending time in these different places. What we want to do is adapt his environment to meet his needs for either stimulation or soothing. We will produce the maximum benefit if we can work with other people, across these different settings, to meet the child's needs.

Finally, although Milieu Therapy and Planned Environment Therapy fell from favour, the idea of the link between the environment and healing is still a valid and valuable one. More and more evidence is emerging from medical and other research that the environment plays a role in healing.

SLIDE 21 Trauma as a model for analysing needs

- Understanding the effects of trauma helps us to analyse the needs of children whose behaviour is causing concern
- Developmental or emotional trauma may lead to diminished ability to:
  - Regulate stress
  - Regulate impulse
  - Process experience through the thinking brain
- If children have difficulty with these functions we can help them through treating them as though they may be traumatised

---

As we have seen, developmental or emotional trauma can leave children unable to cope with stress and prone to rages and impulsive behaviour, because they have not developed the ability to think before they act or to manage their feelings in any other way.

Of course, these are behaviours that we often see in other children and young people too. Some children behave like this even when they have never suffered any kind of developmental or emotional trauma. This kind of behaviour can result from a number of different causes and conditions – for example, a child with attention deficit hyperactivity disorder (ADHD) is also likely to behave impulsively as this is part of the condition.

But whatever the root cause, if children have difficulty with stress and impulse control and processing their experience through thinking, we can help them in the same ways. The same things may help them, whether their problems were caused by trauma or not.

SLIDE 22 Focus on the here and now

- Basing needs analysis on a trauma model makes no assumptions about the child's past
  - It focuses on any difficulties the child may have in physical, emotional, cognitive or social functioning
  - It relates these to known indicators of trauma
- If the difficulties the child shows are similar to those shown by traumatised children, interventions that help victims of trauma may help this child
  - Such interventions cannot do harm to any child
- This does not imply any assumption about the actual experience of the child

---

We will not always know everything about a child's background. We will not always know if a child has suffered trauma, because not all children disclose their experiences. We know that certain difficulties can result from abuse and neglect, but that does not mean that when they are present, abuse and neglect have occurred in every case.

What we are going to do in this session is focus on a child's needs in terms of the physical environment. If a child has not been traumatised but her difficulties are similar to those of traumatised children, these measures will help her too. They certainly will not do any harm.

Treating her as we would treat a traumatised child does not imply that we believes he has suffered trauma.

SLIDE 23   Some examples of indicators suggesting trauma interventions may be useful

- Hyperarousal
  - Aware of discomfort
  - Distressed behaviour
    - Hyperactive
    - Impulsive
    - Poor concentration
    - Aggressive
    - Destructive
    - Self-harm

- Dissociation
  - Split awareness – not aware of discomfort
  - Behaviour may or may not seem distressed
    - Controlling/compliant
    - Withdrawn/artificial
    - Unable to recognise sensory information such as hot/cold
    - Self-harm

This slide shows two lists of behaviours, one associated with hyperarousal and the other with dissociation. Both hyperarousal and dissociation can be the long-term result of childhood trauma – children react in different ways. Hyperarousal is like being on a state of permanent "red alert" to deal with threat – jumpy, easily distracted, easily bored and constantly seeking a high stimulus environment.

Dissociation is a defence mechanism sometimes seen in children who have suffered or witnessed harrowing experiences. It may develop initially as a way of "cutting off" the self from the immediate impact of the stress; but it has longer term harmful effects on the way children function – particularly in relation to other people.

The interventions we are going to discuss will be useful for children showing both of these patterns of behaviours.

SLIDE 24   Using a trauma model to analyse needs

- Think of a child known to you whose behaviour suggests the possibility that the child has difficulty with self-regulation
  - What specific behaviours lead you to this conclusion?
  - Do these behaviours suggest that the child is
    - Hyperaroused?
    - Dissociated?
    - Alternating between the two?
  - What sort of environment does this child most need – SOOTHING? Or STIMULATING?
- Discuss your ideas with others

Exercise

Ask participants to think of a child they know who has difficulties with regulating stress and impulse.

Ask them to think about the questions on Slide 24 and to write down examples of the child's behaviours. Ask for specific examples of behaviour. For example, rather than 'he is unable to tolerate disappointment', you want to know about a specific incident, e.g. 'he threw himself on the floor in the supermarket and screamed when I wouldn't let him have a bar of chocolate'.

Rather than 'he is unable to distinguish between fact and fantasy', you want to know about the time a child stole something from a classmate and then made up a completely different story about what happened and appeared to believe his own story.

Give participants 10 minutes to think about this and make notes, then ask them to discuss what they have written with others on their table or in their small group. Then reconvene the larger group and ask for some examples from participants to share with everyone.

Explain that some types of behaviour point to hyperarousal and others to dissociation. Discuss, as a group, whether the examples you have just heard are likely to be indications of hyperarousal or dissociation. Remind them that a child who is hyperaroused will need a soothing environment; one who is dissociated will need a stimulating environment, at least until he begins to "reconnect".

SLIDE 25   The milieux that have an impact

- Make a list of all the milieux that form part of the environment for the child you have in mind
  - These may include, for example:
    Birth family home/foster home
    Respite care home
    School
    Youth club
    Swimming baths
    Sports hall/community centre
- Which of these do you think are key settings having an impact on stress regulation for the child?

Exercise

Ask participants to do this task as individuals. Point out that a key setting may be important either because of the amount of time the child spends in it, or because it appears to evoke particularly strong reactions.

Listing these milieux is not intended to suggest that they will all be able to adapt in order to meet the needs of traumatised children – it simply assesses the different environments that the child experiences on a day-to-day basis.

Point out that some settings may be surprisingly adaptable.

A school may not be able to make major changes, but even minor changes can make a big difference to the way a traumatised child can manage in a given environment. For instance, the school may be able to set aside a quiet area in the playground or library for children who find it overwhelming and need to be able to retreat from the fray. Schools may not have many looked after children but there are likely to be a number of children who are living with the effects of childhood trauma of one kind or another who would all benefit from changes like this.

SLIDE 26   Assessing the milieux

- Return to the list of key milieux that have an impact on the child you have in mind
- Take one of these settings
- Think your way around it in a sensory tour
  - Remember to consider each of the senses in turn
- What is your assessment of this part of the child's environment in terms of
  Soothing?
  Stimulation?
- Discuss with others and make a note of key points

Exercise

Remind participants of all the sensory information you considered in the previous session that affect a child's experience in a particular environment.

Ask them to consider one of the settings they have just listed and to repeat the exercise of imagining the child making a sensory tour around it. They should consider all five senses, plus other sensory information such as temperature and proximity. While doing this, they should consider whether this setting is soothing or stimulating.

Allow them a few minutes for this task, then ask them to discuss their ideas with others in the small group and the group should jointly make a note of three key points or interesting examples.

Ask each small group to feed these back to the group as a whole.

SLIDE 27   Working with the child to create the healing environment

- Child gains:
  - Insight into own responses
  - Awareness of effects of trauma – normal responses to extreme or dysregulated stress
  - Recognition of need to control self rather than everything else
  - Ability to begin to explain self to others

- Difficulties include:
  - Staying centred when dealing with despairing or controlling child
  - Setting boundaries – adult in control of decisions
  - Working with children with limited communication
  - Working with diversity – class, culture, and so on

Before you show this slide, ask participants the following two questions and encourage them to call out their ideas (write them down on the flipchart):

 Question: How would a child benefit if you involve her when you are creating a more healing environment for her?

Question: What difficulties might it present for you, as a carer, if you involve her in creating a more healing environment?

Some examples of benefits and difficulties are presented on the slide, which you should show after you have heard participants' suggestions. Participants may well have come up with several alternative ideas of their own.

Explain that when working with children on environmental interventions, you should maintain a shared approach and a spirit of 'let's try this and see how it feels'. The carer and child should explore together how different sensory experiences make him feel. The carer needs to look out for the physical effects that follow stimulation and soothing and be aware that the same experience may affect the child differently at different times.

SLIDE 28

Who should be included in planning?

- Thinking again of the chld you have in mind, make a note of everyone you think should be included in planning a healing environment to support the child in recovery from trauma
- Discuss your list with others
- What are the key issues you identify in working with the child and others to promote healing environments in the milieux that have an impact on this child?

Exercise

Ask participants to make a note of people who should be included in planning a healing environment; examples include other members of the family, teachers, social workers, respite carers, therapists, possibly birth family members, leaders of any clubs the child attends – and of course the child himself.

Ask them to discuss their list with others in their small group.

Then ask them to consider the final question on Slide 28 and encourage them to call out their ideas (write them down on the flip chart).

SLIDE 29   Issues in planning the healing environment

- Working with the child
  - **Boundaries** – adults are responsible and in charge
  - **Maintaining equilibrium** – issues of despair and control
- Working with others
  - Clear, open and effective communication
  - Addressing and meeting diverse needs and wishes
  - Managing conflict
- The dynamic quality of recovery
  - Recovery is a journey not an event
  - The needs of the child change – plans must be adaptable

Hopefully, participants will have generated a number of ideas of their own about what they would need to consider when working with the child and others. Now you can show them Slide 29, which lists key issues – which they may or may not have already identified for themselves.

SLIDE 30   Specific changes

- Think of one milieu that has an impact on the child you have in mind
  - Choose a setting in which you know you can make changes
- Make a note of any specific changes that you think would improve the healing properties of the environment for the child
  - Use your handout pack to add to your thinking
  - Consider issues relating to each of the senses in as much detail as possible
  - Small changes can be very powerful
- Discuss your ideas with others and note key points

Exercise

Ask participants to do the tasks listed on Slide 30, first by themselves and then in discussion with others in their small group. They should choose a setting in which they know they can bring about changes, either by themselves or by influencing others.

For instance, they might be aware that the child's respite carers would be particularly receptive to any suggestions about how they could help the child. After hearing about the kind of environment that would be healing for the child, the respite carers may be willing to redecorate or reorganise the child's bedroom.

Or perhaps participants could discuss the ideas about providing a healing environment with the child's teacher, if the teacher is keen to find ways to help the child feel calmer and more settled in the classroom.

Ask participants to think of practical ways to enhance the therapeutic properties of that particular setting. The suggestions on the handout (see article, *About healing environments*, which follows and is also on the CD-ROM) will help. Remind them that even small changes can make a big difference to a child.

If time permits, they should also give some thought to the following:

- Who would be involved in making these changes to the environment?

- How could the changes be put into practice?

- How would you know if the changes are helping?

When they have considered this individually, they should share their ideas with others.

Then ask each small group to present to the group as a whole their ideas for just one of the settings they have been discussing.

SLIDE 31   Planning the environment

- Work with others to produce the outline for a practical plan to make one or more changes that will increase the therapeutic properties of the environment in one milieu that has an impact on the child you have in mind
  - Who will be involved in planning and in implementing the plan?
  - What specific change or changes do you have in mind?
  - How will this be put into practice?
  - By when?
  - How will you know if the change has proved useful?

SLIDE 32   Summary and conclusion

Implications for practice

SLIDE 33   To sum up

- We are affected by our environment through our senses
- Changing the physical environment can help children to recover from trauma
- Soothing environments help children to regulate stress
- Stimulating environments help children to connect and learn
- Even small changes in key milieux can be useful
- It is important to work effectively as a team to promote healing environments for traumatised children

Remind participants of the ground you have covered in this session. Point out that providing the stimulating or soothing environment that will meet the child's needs is likely to involve working in partnership with other significant people in her life. The child will benefit most if people across the various different settings where she spends time recognise the need to make adaptations to create a healing environment for her.

SLIDE 34   Implications for practice

- Please take some time to complete the evaluation form in your pack
- We need your comments on the day, and especially any thoughts or plans you may have to make use of the ideas discussed today in your practice
- If you would like more information on Akamas courses please see our website www.akamas.co.uk

An evaluation form is available on the CD-ROM.

Article

About healing environments

This article is extracted from Working with Traumatised Children
Level 4 BTEC Qualification available online from Akamas
(Also available on the CD-ROM)

Environments that soothe, environments that stimulate

Every sense contributes to the sensory experience that is our constant running interaction with our environment. If there is sensory impairment, then the senses that are active fulfil this function. Even when we are asleep there is some sensory monitoring of our surroundings.

We will now consider in some detail the elements of experience that contribute to the ever-changing sensory map that is our knowledge of the world. Then you will have the opportunity to think about how changes in any of the elements might contribute to healing for a particular child.

Sensory experience that arouses a reaction in the sympathetic nervous system produces stimulation. Sensory experience that reduces arousal in the sympathetic nervous system, and arouses a reaction in the parasympathetic system, produces soothing.

In general, traumatised children are reactive through the sympathetic nervous system, even to stimuli that in others would elicit parasympathetic responses. It is this hypersensitivity that we aim to soothe through environmental changes. When children are disconnected from their own sensory experience through dissociation, however, we may need to help them regain connection before we can help them to soothe the hyperarousal that will result from such connectedness.

When working with children on environmental interventions it is always essential to maintain a shared experimental approach. Explore together with the child the effects of different sensory experience. Be very clear about the physical effects that follow stimulation and soothing. Recognise that the effects of the same experience will be different at different times.

In the notes that follow, a few website references have been included to point you in the direction of useful research. If you are interested you can find much more information via the internet. Try to find academically sound research, such as work being done in universities or hospitals. Many hospitals are now exploring the creative use of the environment to promote healing.

You might also find it interesting to look at the work of Richard Mazuch, Design Director with Nightingales Architects, who specialises in "sense sensitive design" for hospitals and mental health facilities.

Vision

Issues to consider when thinking about what a child experiences visually in an environment include:

- **Light**
  - Natural light or artificial light
  - Full spectrum (like daylight) or part spectrum (like most artificial light)
    - Seasonal Affective Disorder (SAD) is a psychiatric condition affected by changes in daylight and treated through the use of full spectrum light
      - www.nimr.mrc.ac.uk/MillHillEssays/1997/sad.htm
  - Coloured light: bulbs, filters and gels
    - Coloured light has been used effectively with some children with autistic spectrum disorder
      - www.essex.ac.uk/psychology/overlays/
  - Polarised light: sunglasses, windscreens
  - Reflected light and direct light
    - Our ordinary vision comes from reflected light, but television and VDUs involve looking directly at light sources
  - Electric light, gaslight, candlelight, firelight

- **Colour**
  - Walls, ceilings, floors, furnishings, clothes
  - Primary colours, pastel colours, black, white
  - Intensity of colour
  - Combinations of colour
  - Plain or patterned

- **Surfaces**
  - Matt, glossy, absorbing or reflecting light
  - Rough or smooth
  - Natural or synthetic

- **Shape**
  - Straight lines, circles, curves
  - Angular shapes and organic shapes
  - Two dimensions and three dimensions

- **Vista**
  - Short focus or long focus
    - Generally the eye relaxes to longer focus, and when the eye relaxes the body relaxes
    - Movement between short and long focus may be most relaxing
    - Windows, mirrors, three-dimensional objects, and pictures with vistas can all allow the eye to relax

- **Movement within the field of vision**
  - Stillness
  - Gentle movement
  - Hectic movement

- **Images**
  - Natural images
    - Trees, rural scenes, sea, lakes, people, animals, night-time, daytime
  - Constructed images
    - Buildings, mechanical objects, urban scenes
  - Paintings, photographs, murals
    - Art therapy may help traumatised children to connect to their visual sensory experience as well as to express experience through different media

- **Surroundings**
  - Interior space
    - Rooms, corridors
    - Size, shapes, proportions
  - Exterior space
    - Shared entrances, courtyards, gardens, patios
    - Size, shapes, proportions
  - Surrounding landscape
    - Urban, suburban, rural
    - Streets, hills, mountains, moors, fields, lakes, sea

Hearing

Issues to consider when thinking about the sounds a child can hear in an environment include:

- **Ambient sound, the underlying sounds in an environment**
  - Traumatised children may, for example, be sensitive to noise generated by:
    - Refrigerators or freezers
    - Road traffic
    - Trains
    - Aeroplanes
    - Plumbing
    - Other people talking, laughing or singing
    - Background noise from radios and televisions
    - Drills or lawnmowers
      - www.nas.org.uk/nas/jsp/polopoly.jsp?d=297&a=3233

- **Sound quality**
  - Gentle or harsh
  - Loud or soft
  - High pitched or low pitched
  - Pure or complex

- **Music**
  - Type of music
  - Volume: loud or soft
  - Rhythm: rapid or slow
  - Live or recorded
    - Music therapy has been used with children considered to have attachment disorder
      - www.nordoff-robbins.org.uk/html/research.html

- **Voices**
  - Male or female
  - High pitched or low pitched
  - Timbre: the message of the voice quality
  - Familiar language patterns
  - Familiar accents

- **Rhythm**
  - The impact of rhythmic sounds in the environment, such as clocks ticking
  - The use of rhythm such as hand clapping when telling stories or reciting poetry
  - Rhythmic movement to sound, dance

- **Silence**
  - The impact of the absence of sound on the child

Smell and taste

Remember that traumatised children often have reduced function in the thinking brain, the neocortex, and increased function in the reactive and impulsive limbic brain. In that condition they may be hypersensitive to smell and taste. Their senses may be working like the senses of a baby.

Issues to consider in thinking about the smell and taste of an environment include:

- **Basic scent**
  - What are the odours associated with this setting?
    - At home:
      - Entrances, the first smell on entering
      - Living space in the home
      - Bedroom
      - Bathroom
      - Cooking and eating areas
    - At school:
      - Entrances, the first smell on entering
      - Classrooms
      - Changing areas
      - Sports areas
      - Cooking and eating areas
    - At the swimming baths
    - And so on

- **Specific aromas**
  - Natural scents in particular places: plants, flowers, grass, hay
  - Artificial scents: air fresheners, cleaning agents
  - Smells of familiar food
  - Smells of special soothing drinks such as hot chocolate

- **Body odour**
  - Body odour is unique and an important part of the attachment process
    - As children form a positive attachment to their carers the body odour of the carer will become soothing for the child
    - Objects used by the carer may be soothing
      - Clothing such as T-shirts, scarves, gloves
      - Fabric such as pillow cases

- Scent used by a carer may be sprayed on familiar objects such as a school bag or scarf
- Animals
  - If the child forms a relationship with an animal, they may be soothed by carrying something that smells of the animal, such as a small piece of blanket
- Taste
  - What flavours could be associated with the space?
    - Special bedtime drinks
    - Popcorn when watching television
    - Ice cream in the garden

Touch and proxemics

Like smell and taste, the sensory experiences of touch and proximity are very primitive, and may be particularly sensitive in traumatised children.

Remember that dissociated children who are disconnected from their own responses may still be aroused by the sensory experience but unable to recognise the arousal. So hyperaroused children are unable to regulate the arousal, and dissociated children are unable either to recognise or to regulate the arousal.

Issues to be considered when thinking about what a child experiences in the environment in terms of touch and proxemics include:

- **Texture of walls, floors, objects**
  - We are in touch with our physical environment more than we usually realise. People can orientate themselves in space by the texture of familiar floors, for example:
    - Natural or synthetic material
    - Rough or smooth
    - Soft or hard
    - Felt with the hands, feet, or whole body

- **Surfaces of furniture, floors, objects**
  - Every physical thing has a surface, and every surface may be touched. The nature of the surface will determine whether for any person the touch is stimulant or soothing
    - Natural or synthetic material
    - Rounded or sharp-edged
    - Straight lines or organic forms
    - Hard or soft

- **Temperature**
  - Cold, warm or hot
  - Comfortable or uncomfortable

- **Fabrics**
  - Babies love to stroke fabrics, and so do many traumatised children
    - Natural or synthetic material
    - Rough or smooth
    - Soft or stiff and unyielding
    - Plain or with holes and patterns
    - Felt with hands, feet, or whole body

- **Water**
  - Water can be very frightening for some traumatised children, especially if they were abused in bathrooms, but it can also be very soothing
    - Cold, warm or hot
    - Still (like a bath) or moving (like a shower)
    - Deep or shallow
    - Rain and snow, and other outdoor water

- **Moving air**
  - Traumatised children often respond to moving air
    - Fans
    - Hairdryers
    - Wind in the open air

- **Skin, hair and fur**
  - Contact with other humans or animals can be stimulant or soothing
    - Touching other people
    - Doing hair for other people
    - Stroking animals

- **Pillows, cushions and duvets**
  - Children and young people will often hug a pillow or cushion, or snuggle into a duvet
    - Size and shape
    - Firm or yielding
    - Nature of covering fabric

- **Proxemics**
  - Areas of the environment where people are brought close together by the architecture or the arrangement of furniture
    - Traumatised children often find closeness threatening
  - Areas of the environment where people are kept far apart by the architecture or the arrangement of furniture
    - Children who are beginning to form attachments may find distance frightening
  - Areas where people are brought face-to-face
    - Eye contact is stimulant, and many traumatised children cannot manage it
  - Areas where people are side by side, or facing in different directions
    - Traumatised children often feel more comfortable when close to but not face-to-face with others. On the other hand they may just feel disorientated.

References

American Psychological Association (1994) *Diagnostic and Statistical Manual of Mental Disorders* (4th edition), Washington, DC: American Psychiatric Association

Bettelheim B (1974) *A Home for the Heart*, London: Thomas & Hudson

Bronfenbrenner U (1979) *The Ecology of Human Development: Experiments by nature and design*, Cambridge, MA: Harvard University Press

Daniel B and Wassell S (2002a) *The Early Years: Assessing and promoting resilience in vulnerable children 1*, London: Jessica Kingsley

Daniel B and Wassell S (2002b) *The School Years: Assessing and promoting resilience in vulnerable children 2*, London: Jessica Kingsley

Daniel B and Wassell S (2002c) *Adolescence: Assessing and promoting resilience in vulnerable children 3*, London: Jessica Kingsley

Gilligan R (2001) *Promoting Resilience: A resource guide on working with children in the care system*, London: BAAF

Jackson S (2001) *Nobody Ever Told us School Mattered: Raising the educational attainments of children in care*, London: BAAF

Janoff-Bulman R (1992) *Shattered Assumptions: Towards a new psychology of Trauma*, New York: The Free Press

Kohlberg (ref to come)

van der Kolk *et al* (1996) *Traumatic Stress: The effects of overwhelming experience on mind, body and society*, New York: The Guilford Press

Office of the United Nations High Commission for Human Rights (1990) *Convention on the Rights of the Child*, Geneva: Office of the United Nations